Tassajara Cooking

by Edward Espe Brown

Introduction by Richard Baker-roshi

Shambhala

Berkeley · London

1973

A Zen Center Book

SHAMBHALA PUBLICATIONS, INC.
1409 Fifth Street
Berkeley, California 94710
and
Barn Cottage
Stert, Devizes
Wiltshire

ISBN 0-87773-046-6 (cloth)
ISBN 0-87773-047-4 (paper)
LCC 73-86144
Printed in the United States of America
by Banta-Levison Co., Reno, Nevada

This is a *Zen Center Book*, produced by members
of the Zen Center community, in cooperation
with Shambhala Publications, Inc. For further
information about Zen Center, please write:
Zen Center, 300 Page Street, San Francisco,
California 94102.

Distributed in the Commonwealth and Europe
by Routledge & Kegan Paul, Ltd.
London and Henley-on-Thames

ACKNOWLEDGING that many people wrote this book: Fortunately, no one
has to do everything —
     Suzuki-roshi revealed the ground. "What will you do now?" he asked.
     Tim Buckley played the part of editor, reader, producer, consultant, friend,
poet. Blessings.
     Robert Lytle made coffee, babysat, typed, indexed, and edited copy.
     Meg birthed and nursed our baby and our garden, cooked, laundered,
shopped, and otherwise put up with her husband-turned-writer.
     Del Carlson did the illustrations—which was what got me started writing.
Dan Welch drew Tassajara cooking, and Bob Boni photographed the cabbage.
Haru and Andrew Main set type; Hal Hershey and Red Dog Pieface designed
the book and laid it out. Sam Bercholz at Shambhala gave his interest,
encouragement, advice and confidence.
     Arthur Mayeno lay in traction, working on the lettering for the cover.
Rebecca took care of him. If they could do that, I could write.
     Many Zen Center cooks, past and present, contributed recipes and
experience. Gassho.
     Baker-roshi saw us through it all.
     My respect and gratitude for everybody's efforts.

Introduction

By Zentatsu Baker-roshi

Food is our common property, the body of the world, our eating
of the world, our treasure of change and transformation, sustenance
and continuation. It is the essence of Buddha's mind and practice,
the unfathomable effort of all beings who have brought us this
time to eat from most ancient times, from every world, past and
present. It is the countless other creatures that constantly help.
It is the water, sunlight, and turning of the earth. It is our absorp-
tion of the suffering of the plants and creatures eaten, or displaced
or killed by clearing and harvesting. It is cooking and eating,
preparation and cleaning, planting and sewage, exchanging and
transporting.

Thus our parents and teachers have transmitted their bodies
and minds to us to continue the realization of the Dharma this
very moment.

> Homage to the Buddhas and Bodhisattvas
> and to the countless beings
> for this food and teaching.

Dogen-zenji said, "We must care for food as if it is our own eye-
sight." And he said, "If one is moved by things and people, one
is also able to move them. The pure actions of the cook must come
forth from his realization of the unity of all things and beings; and
by seeing clearly into the minds and hearts of others, from a leaf
of cabbage he must be able to produce a sixteen-foot Buddha."

This cooking book is about food and cooking, and Ed Brown,
Zen Center, and Buddhist practice.

Green Gulch Zen Farm
Summer 1973

Cooking is not a mystery.
The more heart we put out
the more heart we put in.
To bring cooking alive
we give our life. Giving
our life willingly we don't
get put out.
Washing cutting cooking cleaning,
exploring ways to give life to our life.
Not knowing already how and what to do,
practice feeling it
out of what is not known
through the warmth and anxiety,
not sticking to a particular way,
insisting it is the only way
even though it is quite good;
open to feeling the various possibilities,
the tentative ways of giving life to our life.

To feel out our left hand, our back, our toes,
to feel out our breathing, our movements, our stance,
this is our freedom, this is our wisdom.
The mystery is that it is possible to do
what we don't know how to do.

Contents

Dedicated to —

Pumpkin

    Carrot

        Cabbage

Potato

    Radish

        Beans

The Ground

    which gives

        Life

Beginning

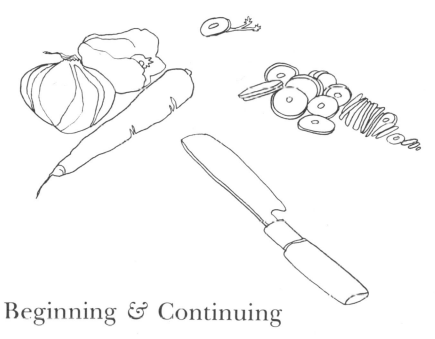

Beginning & Continuing

You follow recipes, you listen to advice, you go your own way.
Even wholehearted effort sometimes falls short, the best intentions
do not insure success. There is no help for it, so go ahead, begin
and continue: with yourself, with others, with vegetables.

Begin and continue with what is in front of you.

The way to be a cook is to cook. The results don't have to be
just right, measuring up to some imagined or ingrained taste. Our
cooking doesn't have to prove how wonderful or talented we are.
Our original worth is not something which can be measured,
increased or decreased. Just feed, satisfy, nourish. Enter each
activity thoroughly, freshly, vitally. Splash! There is completely
no secret: just plunging in, allowing time, making space, giving
energy, tending each situation with warm-hearted effort. The
spoon, the knife, the food, the hunger; broken plates and broken
plans. Play, don't work. Work it out.

1

The Knife

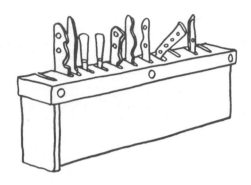

If you're interested in preparing vegetables with some proficiency, get a good knife, keep it sharp, and learn how to use it. An inexpensive paring knife, although it's better than nothing, will not do a good job in general kitchen use. The knife you see in most of the pictures in this book is a Japanese vegetable knife. This is, simply,

a fantastic knife for cutting vegetables, because it is made solely for that purpose. A "chef's knife," with its curving blade, makes an excellent alternative. Chef's knives come in several lengths, but seven inches is plenty long enough for home use.

The chef's knife, like most Japanese vegetable knives, is made of carbon steel rather than stainless steel. Carbon steel blades sharpen quite easily, while stainless steel knives cannot be sharpened as readily. Stainless steel does, however, hold its edge longer, and also has the advantage of not reacting with the acids in some foods. This is especially important

when working with fruits and the more acidy vegetables, such as tomatoes.

2

Cutting

Cutting takes a knife, a cutting surface at a comfortable height, something to cut, a steady rhythm in the cutting hand, an open eye in the guiding hand. Do some patient, steady practicing and sharpen your mind as well as the knife.

I am going to describe a rather detailed approach to cutting. Even though you don't cut exactly according to these instructions, they may give you some idea of what the possibilities are.

The right hand cuts, the left hand guides. Given the opportunity, hands can see quite well for themselves, so the eyes needn't be too involved.

We are usually pretty handy with our right hand and awkward with our left, so the key to fast, efficient, effortless cutting is to develop the capacity of the left hand to hold, manage, and manipulate the vegetables, while it guides the knife with the last knuckle of its middle finger. The right hand just cuts.

The left hand: Every joint is bent, and the fingertips are carefully, mindfully, continually tucked back. This way no fingertips interfere with the knife stroke. Ouch!

The thumb and last finger are usually used to grip the sides of the vegetable, while the other three fingers are curled, resting

on top. The last knuckle of the middle finger will be the principle guide for the knife, so that knuckle is the furthest extension of the left hand.

About guiding the knife: Keep your right hand dumb. It's just going to cut cut cut, always guided by the last knuckle of the middle finger of the left hand. Either the left hand walks back along the vegetable, the knife following, moving over just as far as the retreating knuckle, or the left hand inches the vegetable forward, maintaining its own position.

Especially when cutting leafy greens, parsley, green onions and so forth, the left hand is also used to keep the ends together in a position to be cut.

Now the right hand: The knife is held with the thumb and first finger gripping the sides of the blade, just past the handle. The remaining fingers grip the handle. Try it. A slight motion of the fingers and wrist controls the blade's movement.

With knife in hand there are various possible strokes, and there are some principles that are applicable to all of them: Hold the blade perpendicular to the cutting surface, in a comfortable position in front of you. Diagonal slices are made by holding the vegetables at an acute angle to the knife, not by changing the knife's position. Another general principle is to incorporate at least some sawing motion into the slice or chop. Sawing means the knife is in motion forward or backward as well as down. Try to saw with each slice or chop. In this case *"chopping"* means to cut mostly up-down with a slight saw, and *"slicing"* means to cut mostly back and forth with some up-down feeling. You can use whichever method works best for the particular vegetable you are working with. (Later when the directions say to "slice" or "section," it means slice or chop as you prefer.)

4

Two Ways to Slice:

In slicing, the tip (or curve) of the knife is kept on the cutting surface, while the rest of the knife is raised. The cut is made by pulling the knife toward you and down, then returning it to the poised position (see *Green Onions*.) Or the cut can be made by pushing the knife away from you and down, then returning the knife to the raised position (see *Slicing Carrots into Matchsticks*).

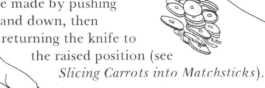

Three Ways to Chop:

Down and slightly forward. Return. (See *Celery*.)

Down and slightly forward, continuing down and slightly back. Return. A circular feeling. (See *Potatoes*.)

Down and slightly towards you. Return. (See *Radishes*.)

The pictures show my accustomed way of cutting. My experience is that slicing works well with smaller (narrower) things. As the size increases, I find that I prefer to chop more. For instance, I slice the narrow end of carrots and chop the fatter end.

At first your right hand will be very speedy, but slow it down to the pace set by the guiding left hand. Cut steadily, evenly, rhythmically, letting speed come with practice.

The trick is to be willing to try, not to heed that voice which says: "This is too hard" or "I could never cut like that!" Give your hands several chances. In fact, don't put any limit on the number of chances.

Care & Feeding of Knives

Sharpening

Dull knives make cutting difficult. Also they are more dangerous than sharp ones. More pressure must be exerted when using them, hence less control is possible—the added force is easily put into cutting the cook as well as the vegetable. A sharp knife, on the other hand, cuts cleanly and readily, so you don't end up hacking away at things and having the knife bounce off the vegetable and into your hand.

The stone: Since various knife sharpening gizmos are self-explanatory, the sharpening instructions here concentrate on how to use a flat sharpening stone. Working with such a stone is a fine way to get close and familiar with your knife, as well as getting it sharp. Different kinds of stones are available, the most common being man-made—Emory (India Stone) or Carborundum. These stones often come with two grits bonded together, back to back—a coarser one for roughing down and a finer one for finishing (honing) the edge. Natural Arkansas stone is harder, faster and far more expensive. It is especially useful for sharpening stainless steel and for final razor-sharp honing. For most kitchen knives, however, a large Carborundum stone—8″ by 2″ by 1″ is a common size—will be quite adequate.

Oil: All stones must be used with a *light* oil. Kerosene is excellent. "3 in 1" or baby oil are fine. "Honing Oil" is unnecessarily expensive, and vegetable oil is not good for this purpose. The oil suspends the minute metal filings, keeping them from filling up the grit of the stone. When you're sharpening well, the oil will turn black with metal filings steadily and rapidly. Be moderate with the oil, but not stingy, and wipe the stone dry when finished so that it doesn't get gummy.

Sharpening: Vegetables can be best cut with a very finely angled edge, rather than the steeply angled one needed to hold up against bone and gristle. So when sharpening a knife for vegetable cutting, keep the angle between blade and stone at about 5° or less. The grinding process will then leave a shiny strip about an eighth of an inch wide along the edge of the blade—all the way, evenly, from haft to tip. If there are scratches farther up the sides of the blade,

6

the knife has been held too flat against the stone.

Sharpening is a matter of touch and personal style, but if you haven't sharpened knives before, here's a technique to get you started: Have the oiled stone on a steady surface at a comfortable working height. Place the edge of the knife against the surface of the stone at a shallow angle and begin "slicing" the top of the stone—very thin slices! Do this by either drawing the knife across the surface while also moving it from one end toward the other, one knife-length per stroke, or by moving the knife in small circles as you go down the stone. When you reach the end of the stone, turn the blade over and bring it back towards you, sharpening one side of the edge and then the other.

With a large knife it may be easiest to use both hands, moving the blade with the right and applying pressure with the left. Use only enough pressure to keep the edge in contact with the stone, and to turn the oil black at a reasonable rate. Sharpening is much more a matter of time and patience than of force. Remember too, that dull knives will take much longer to sharpen than those touched up regularly. To check on your progress, hold the knife in front of you with its edge up, so that the light catches the very edge. Move the edge back and forth in the light. Any bright spots? A sharp edge will reflect practically no light, while a reflection shows a flatness. If there are "flats," sharpen some more, concentrating on those spots. How's the tip? When the edge looks and feels pretty good, finish it on the finer grit or stone.

Caring for Knives

It will be to your, and your knife's, advantage not to leave it lying about, especially not amongst all the other clutter in the sink or in a drawer where you can't always know when you're about to come up against its sharpness, and where the edge will be quickly lost against other hard objects. There are various kinds of knife racks which keep knives sharp and out of harm's way. Also, no time or energy lost looking. It's right there.

Clean knives carefully before putting them away, using a rag or a sponge or your hand, not a scouring pad, and dry them off. A bit of vegetable oil rubbed into a carbon-steel knife will keep it from getting rusty, and helps keep the tarnishing down. Makes it feel good, too.

Cooking Methods

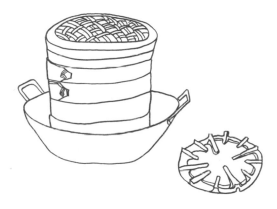

If you are going to cook vegetables rather than eat them raw, there are usually several possible ways, and combinations of ways, to do it. Here are some different methods of cooking—at least my definitions of the various terms, the way they are used in this book.

(It is best to figure out which method you'll be using before you begin cutting the vegetables.)

Sautéing

I use this word to mean frying vegetables in oil, usually over high heat. Technically the vegetables are being *sautéed* only if they are dry and each piece has continuous, or at least quite frequent, contact with the bottom of the pan. If the vegetables are piled up, the ones on top are "steaming."

The way I like to "sauté" is a variation of the Chinese stir-frying technique: First the pan is heated, then oil is added. A little oil will go a long way here because the hot pan thins it out. Salt is sprinkled on the oil and roasted momentarily before the vegetables are added. The vegetables are tossed and stirred, so that each is coated with the salted oil and none burn. The hot oil and the heat of the pan will work to seal in the juices of the vegetables, but at the same time the salt will be drawing out some moisture from the interior of the vegetable, giving each piece a moist juiciness.

9

Sautéing is often a first step in combination with steaming, simmering or baking.

Fry or *Sear:* This is the same as sautéing, or stir-frying, without the stirring or tossing. Some browning is meant to take place. For this method, though, no salt is sprinkled on the oil.

Sauté-steam: This will work well with medium-sized pieces of almost any vegetable, especially those which need added moisture, such as peas. The vegetable is first sautéed as above for three to four minutes, then a small amount of liquid—water, stock, soy sauce— is added and the pan covered with a close-fitting lid. When the liquid is boiling, possibly immediately, turn the heat down so that it just maintains the boiling, low enough anyway so that the vegetables don't burn while they're steaming. The steaming takes just about four to eight minutes for most things.

Sauté-simmer: The vegetables are sautéed for three to four minutes, and then put in a simmering liquid for further cooking, either immediately or later. The simmering part will take ten to twenty minutes, or longer if the liquid needs to be heated. The preliminary sautéing gives the vegetables a toasted, nutty flavor, and total cooking time is less than for straight simmering.

One way to cook vegetables ahead of time and still have them come out well is to put sautéed vegetables in sauce over low heat, or if nearly done, to put the vegetables with sauce in a double boiler, or in a slow oven.

Sauté-bake: Vegetables may be first sautéed and then put in a baking dish in the oven to complete their cooking. With some liquid and a lid, the vegetables can steam in the oven. (See Oven Use for more information.) The baking part is likely to take at least fifteen to twenty minutes. The sauté-bake is another suitable way of getting vegetables prepared before the last-minute rush.

Simmering or Stewing

This means that the vegetables are cooking in some kind of liquid in which just a few bubbles are popping to the surface here and there. It is more gentle than boiling, where the whole surface is rolling.

Boiling

The vegetables cook in some boiling liquid. I often use this expression to mean boiling in the French manner: The water or stock is salted, one-half teaspoon salt to one quart liquid, and heated to boiling. Then the vegetables are added, the pot covered, and the heat left on high at least until the liquid returns to boiling. Turn the heat down to a gentle rolling boil rather than a raging boil. The vegetables will be best if they are taken out when verging on tenderness, rather than after they are tender, since they continue cooking even after being removed from the water. If the vegetables and liquid are poured into a strainer or a colander set in another pot, the cooking liquid can be saved for soup or cereal or bread, or another batch of 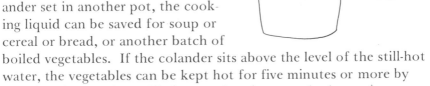 boiled vegetables. If the colander sits above the level of the still-hot water, the vegetables can be kept hot for five minutes or more by covering them. They will also stay hot for several minutes in a covered serving bowl.

Boiling is wasteful of nutrients and flavor *unless* the cooking liquid is saved. Adele Davis bets that not one housewife in a million saves the liquid, but I personally know several who do, including one whose family drinks it for juice.

Steaming

The vegetables cook in steam if they are above some steaming liquid in a closed pot. They will be steaming only slightly if the pot is open and the steam is escaping. The steaming liquid can be vegetable juices, stock, or water. The vegetables are above the steaming liquid if they are on top of other vegetables, or if they are on some kind of rack made of metal, or perhaps bamboo.

Sprinkle salt on the vegetables once they are in the steamer or on top of the other vegetables.

11

Oven Use

When something is cooking in the oven, we generally call it "baking." However, it is helpful to realize that all the other techniques of cooking which have been discussed can happen in the oven as well as on top of the stove. If a vegetable like a potato, for instance, is cut up, the pieces brushed with oil and baked, it amounts to an oven "fry." Vegetables in a covered baking dish with a small amount of liquid will be steaming. Likewise vegetables in a sauce or liquid can be simmering or boiling in the oven. So the oven may be quite useful in keeping the top of the stove a little less cluttered and busy at the last minute.

Braising

This means that the food is half covered with liquid and simmering-steaming in the oven.

Salting Vegetables

Salt draws the liquid out of vegetables. This may be done for several possible reasons: it softens, preserves (pickles) and, as in the case of eggplant, mellows. If a moderate amount of salt is used, the drawn liquid can often be used for dressing, soups, or sauces.

Here's the way the salting is done: The vegetables are cut up and sprinkled with salt, just about as much as if you were going to eat them. Then some weight is applied to the salted vegetables. If they are in a bowl, a smaller plate or bowl is put on top of the vegetables and a weight of some sort on top of that. The weight used can be a stone, a heavy pot, a large jar of peanut butter. This is arranged so that, as the vegetables soften and condense, the plate on top pushes farther down. The pressure is an added help to salt and time.

Vegetables are usually salted for one-half hour to several hours, but in some cases can be left for months.

Crushing Herbs

Fresh herbs are wonderful, but I don't seem to have found myself next door to that many herb gardens, so usually I've made do with dried herbs. These come either "whole" or "ground." Ground herbs get stale even faster than whole dried herbs. Use whole dried herbs

 by crushing them between the palm of one hand and the fleshy part of the other. A mortar and pestle is also good for crushing herbs, and it is an effective way to crush and grind seeds used for seasoning, such as cumin, anise, fennel, coriander, and cardamom.

Dissolving Cornstarch

One tablespoon of cornstarch thickens a cup of liquid. Here is how it is done: The cornstarch is dissolved in a small amount of cold water, since if it meets directly with hot liquid, lumps will form. Cornstarch does its thickening when the liquid containing it is boiled. Have the main body of liquid boiling, and then pour in the dissolved cornstarch, stirring immediately. Right away the cornstarch cooks and thickens. No problem. The problem, if there is one, is that cornstarch very quickly begins to settle, so if it doesn't cook upon being added to the boiling liquid, keep stirring until it does. Also be sure to stir up the dissolved cornstarch just before adding it to the hot liquid.

Plants

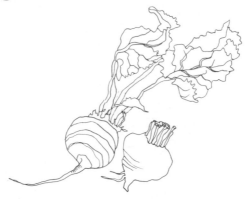

In this book vegetables are grouped first by the season in which they reach maturity, and second by what part of the plant is the edible portion: *root, stem, leaves, fruit,* or *bud.* The seasonal classification is rather arbitrary since, with modern methods of production and transportation, many more vegetables are available in more places more often. Included as *Year Round* foods are those vegetables most readily available, and those vegetables maturing in late summer and fall which can be fairly easily kept through the winter.

The *Cool Weather* vegetables are those which bolt to seed in hot weather. Some areas of California are cool enough in the summer and warm enough in the winter that these vegetables can be grown almost year round, while other areas may produce one fall crop or one spring crop. Included in this category are some root vegetables, asparagus, all of the bud vegetables, and most of the leafy vegetables. Collard greens, which grow well in hot weather, are included under Greens (cool weather) for cooking purposes.

Grouped as *Summer Vegetables* are all of the "fruit" crops, those which form after the flower and which contain seeds and seed-food. These vegetables need heat to mature their fruit. Peas, the first of the fruit crops, can't take as much sun as the others. Green beans also come fairly early, and then all the others come in.

Vegetables available at the same time of year generally combine well with each other or make companionable dishes. They will be cheapest and at their best during their prime season.

To think about what part of the plant each vegetable is may help to determine how it can best be prepared. There are exceptions, but root vegetables generally take the most cooking, and leafy vegetables take the least. Then, too, root vegetables are earthy, leafy vegetables more airy, and fruit vegetables more full of sun: accordingly, heaviness, lightness, or warmth can be added to a dish or meal, and consideration may be given to having some of each at each meal or in the course of a week.

Vegetables are, of course, classified biologically, and occasionally some reference is made to a vegetable's familial relationship in this book. By far the largest "family" of vegetables are the mustards: broccoli, cauliflower, Brussels sprouts, cabbage, kale, turnips, rutabagas, kohlrabi, and mustard greens are all in this family, as are radishes, watercress, and peppercress. These vegetables all develop a "boiled cabbage" flavor when overcooked. Also of interest is the fact that asparagus, along with onion, leek, and garlic, is a member of the lily family.

	Year Round	Spring & Fall (Cool Weather)	Summer
ROOTS & TUBERS	Carrot Onion Potato Sweet Potato Yams Garlic Ginger	Turnip Rutabaga Radishes Beets	

SHOOTS, LEAVES & STEMS	Green Onion
	Celery
	Cabbage
	Parsley
		Asparagus (spring only)
		Lettuces
		Greens:
		  Spinach
		  Chard
		  Kale
		  Mustard
			Collards (see Greens)

BUDS		Broccoli Cauliflower Artichoke	

FRUITS	Winter Squashes:
	  Acorn
	  Hubbard
	  Banana
			Pea
			Snow Pea
			Green Beans
			Tomato
			Cucumber
			Summer Squashes:
			  Zucchini
			  Crookneck
			  Scalloped
			Eggplant
			Sweet Corn
			Avocado

ORDER	"Family" (group)* Vegetable, *Genus*		
GRASS	"Grass" Corn, *Zea*		
LILY	"Lily" Asparagus, *Asparagus;* Garlic, *Allium;* Leek, *Allium;* Onion, *Allium*		
BUCKWHEAT	"Buckwheat" Rhubard, *Rheum;* Sorrel, *Rumex;* Dock, *Rumex*		
GOOSEFOOT	"Goosefoot" Beet, *Beta;* Chard, *Beta;* Spinach, *Spinacea*		
POPPY	"Mustard" Broccoli, *Brassica;* Brussels Sprouts, *Brassica;* Cabbage, *Brassica;* Cauliflower, *Brassica;* Kale, *Brassica;* Kohlrabi, *Brassica;* Mustard, *Brassica;* Rutabaga, *Brassica;* Turnip, *Brassica;* Pepper Cress, *Lepidium;* Radish, *Raphanus;* Watercress, *Roripa*		
ROSE	"Pulse" Bean, *Phaseolus;* Broadbean, *Vicia;* Soybean, *Glycine;* Lentil, *Lens;* Pea, *Pisum*		
MALLOW	"Mallow" Okra, *Hibiscus*		
PARSLEY	"Parsley" Carrot, *Daucus;* Celeriac, *Apium;* Celery, *Apium;* Parsley, *Petroselineum;* Parsnip, *Pastinaca*		
PHLOX	"Morning Glory" Sweet Potato, *Ipomea* "Nightshade" Eggplant, *Solanum;* Potato, *Solanum;* Pepper, *Capiscum;* Tomato, *Lycopersicum*		
MADDER	"Valerian" Corn Salad (Lamb's Quarters), *Valerianella*		
GOURD	"Gourd" Cucumber, *Cucumis;* Muskmelon, *Cucumis;* Water- melon, *Citrullus;* Gourd, *Lagenaria;* Pumpkin, *Cuscurbita;* Squashes, *Cuscurbita*		
BELLFLOWER	"Composite"		
	(chicory)	Chicory, *Chichorium;* Endive, *Chichorium;* Dandelion, *Taraxacum;* Lettuce, *Lactuca;* Salisfy, *Tragopogon*	
	(sunflower)	Jerusalem Artichoke, *Helianthus*	
	(thistle)	Artichoke, *Cynara*	

*Applies only to the great composite family.

17

When Are Vegetables?

Take a look at what needs to be used. Keep in mind what's in the refrigerator, and start with the oldest vegetables.

When are the vegetables still good? Vegetables are still good up to, but not including, the point at which they become rotten. If not too far along, the slimy parts can be removed. Greens are on their way when yellow. These are vegetables at their worst. Lacking in appetizing appearance, they can still go into a bean soup, or perhaps be cooked and mashed and then put in soups, or served with a complementary (cover-up) sauce. Vegetables on the edge of oblivion have often been noted to add a marvelous, distinctive taste to casseroles, soups, and mixed vegetable dishes. Play it by nose.

The next class of vegetables are those wilted or limp from loss of water. These too can still be used. They will need little doctoring other than the addition of some form of liquid—a sauce, a dressing, a light soup. In this way limp vegetables often make do for nearly any use.

When vegetables are in their prime, consider doing as little as possible. Consider letting them be what they are, rather than making them something else. Hopefully, the simple recipes that follow will prove a guide for doing just this.

Of course, once in a great while vegetables do become un-eatable. Careful planning and consideration can keep such loss to a minimum, but when it occurs, please give the vegetables back to Mother, via a compost pile. Sometimes, even botched cooking must end up there, but when is a dish really botched? Here's the recipe for some of the finest greens I ever ate. I don't necessarily recommend that you try to duplicate this recipe, but maybe you will sometime without even trying.

Smoked Greens

greens   lemon butter   oil   salt

The greens were cooked in a *wok,* the concave Chinese frying pan, over a high flame. They were briefly forgotten about until—Oh no! They're burning! Complete dismay in the kitchen—forty people waiting for supper—just have to make do. The blackened greens stuck to the bottom of the pan, and out came the rest, to be served with lemon-flavored butter. Everyone wondered, "How did the greens get this wonderful smoked flavor, as though they'd been cooked with some mighty fine ham?" C'est la vie.

And then all of those blackened leaves had to be cleaned out of the pan.

Cooking Vegetables

Whatever is done will not make a cucumber
more of a cucumber or a radish more of a radish.
Cucumber is cucumber, radish is radish.
What is done may make a vegetable more suitable
to some particular taste—that's the usual way,
to see what taste we want. But why not
ask the cucumber, why not ask the radish?
What is the taste it would like to express?

Vegetables Themselves

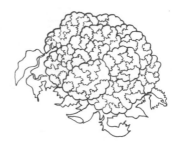

Preparing things simply is deceptively difficult, since there is no way to cover up our mistakes.

When food is always fancy or elaborate, then fanciness becomes quite ordinary, and we forget the plain, full-natured, actual taste of things. Living in a world of created taste, we think that we can make everything suit our fancy. We reject foods which do not suit our cultivated taste, which gets increasingly particular the more we cater to it. Soon enough we have quite a low level of tolerance, of willingness to experience the unfamiliar. When we are not so particular, not always comparing a particular taste with what we are used to, then we can experience and appreciate the actual taste of things. They won't always taste like we thought they would, but they may still be quite tasty.

On the other hand: Vegetables used to drive me crazy, up the wall. I couldn't stand them. The very sound of the word evoked something frightfully distasteful. "At least *try* it" was always the command, on occasion reluctantly obeyed. I mainly ate frozen peas and frozen green beans. Then in eighth grade a girl made a Show-and-Tell salad with sour cream and basil dressing. That's when I started eating lettuce. When I was in high school, my mother cooked cabbage with wine, and that's when I started eating cabbage. Since then my vocabulary of edible vegetables has increased enormously. Only Brussels sprouts give me pause, but I cook and eat them anyway.

The recipes in this section have very few measurements. There are several reasons for this, but basically I am crediting everyone with an ability to sense things out for themselves. The size of vegetables varies, appetites vary, tastes vary. Numbers can be fairly arbitrary. If you like onions, put more in; if you don't like carrots, use less. "Spinach with Onion and Carrot" could be "Onion with Carrot and Spinach" or "Carrot with Spinach and Onion."

Vegetables can be cooked much more precisely by taste and experience than they can by numbers. You know very quickly how full the salad bowl needs to be to serve everyone, which bowl (or combination of bowls) needs filling in order to make a vegetable dish. Cook more when it's a dish you and your family just love and can't get enough of. Cook less when it's a dish that people aren't so fond of, or perhaps one that you're trying out for the first time.

You're the cook. What I call "cooked" may be someone's "half raw." It's a tentative designation. What I call "overcooked" may be someone's favorite way of preparation. Don't cook for me, cook for yourself, and for those who will be eating.

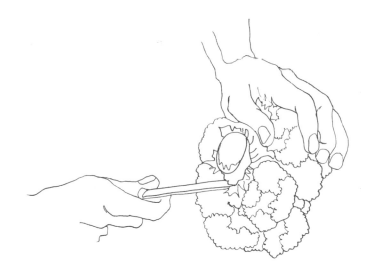

Winter & Year 'Round

Carrots

Quite common and ordinary, carrots are also versatile, cheap, and too-often neglected. They can be prepared deliciously by themselves, and add sweetness and color when grated in salads, combined with other vegetables, or added to soups.

   Carrots are used here to exemplify several possible vegetable cuts. Any one shape can be done in different sizes. I almost never peel carrots, but do scrub them thoroughly and then cut off the stem and root tail.

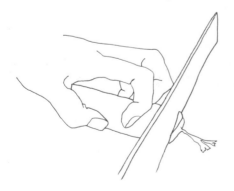

   Rounds or Ovals: The cutting can start at either end of the carrot. Use the forward-back, tip-of-the-knife-down stroke, or one of the up-down chopping cuts. The latter is particularly effective at the carrot's thick end. For rounds the cut is made straight across the carrot, and for ovals the cut is made diagonally across the carrot. For ovals, keep the knife in the same position as when cutting straight across but change the angle of the carrot. *(See illustrations, p. 4-5.)*

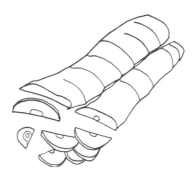

Halfmoons:
Cut the carrot in half lengthwise. Slice.

Dicing:
Leaving the carrot intact
at the fatter end, make
two or three cuts length-
wise, then, perpendicular
to these cuts, make two
or three more cuts.
Cut the "squid" carrot
crosswise to dice.
Diced carrots can
also be made by
cutting large
matchstick pieces
crosswise.

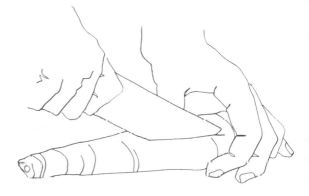

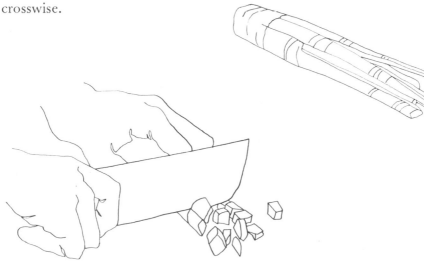

25

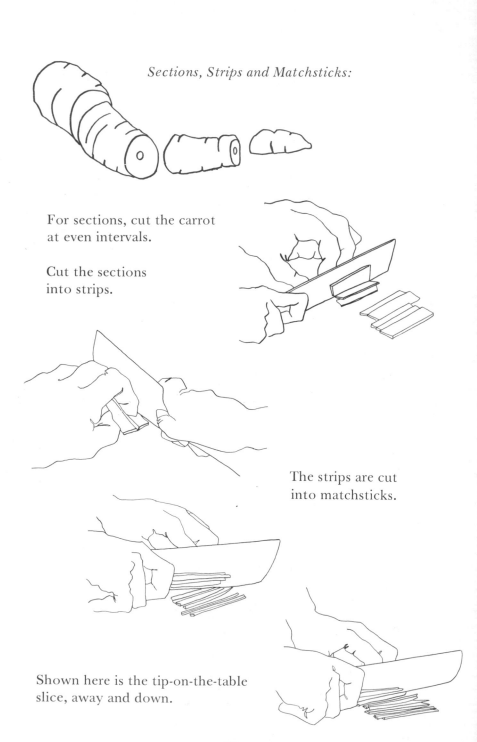

Sections, Strips and Matchsticks:

For sections, cut the carrot
at even intervals.

Cut the sections
into strips.

The strips are cut
into matchsticks.

Shown here is the tip-on-the-table
slice, away and down.

26

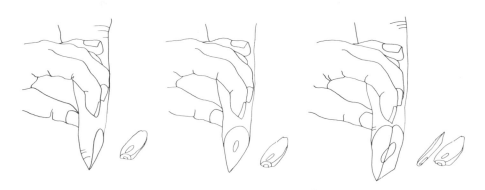

Chinese rolling cut: After each diagonal cut the carrot is rotated by walking your fingertips towards you. Each cut intersects the plane of the preceding cut. These pieces can be made large or small, fatter, thinner, longer, shorter.

Carrot Salad   earthy and chewy

carrot   salt   lemon

Wash and grate the carrot. Sprinkle with salt and lemon juice. Mix well. Two variations: carrot salad with raisins or dates, nuts and apple. Carrot salad with raw turnip, green onion and nuts.

Breakfast Carrots   (good anytime)

Just carrots cooked with oil and salt. Without fancy ideas in mind, they taste pretty fine.

carrots   oil   salt   water or stock

Wash and slice carrots in rounds or ovals, or use the rolling cut. Stir-fry for three to four minutes, until the sizzling quiets down. Add a couple of tablespoons of water, put on a close fitting lid and turn the heat down moderately low. Cook about six minutes with the lid on. Are they done? Salt to taste. When the breakfast carrots are ready, you might add toasted nuts or seeds, or maybe wheat germ.

Sweet & Sour Dinner Carrots

These carrots start out like Breakfast Carrots and then become Dinner Dinner Carrots.

carrots   oil   salt   dates (or raisins)
lemon juice and water   (nuts if you wish)

Wash and cut the carrots. Section the dates. Cook as in Breakfast Carrots, only when it's time to add the water, add half water and half lemon juice, plus the dates or raisins, and the nuts.

Sauced Sweet & Sour Carrots

1 t oil
1 t tomato sauce or catsup
1 t sherry
¼ t powdered ginger, or
* ½ t grated fresh ginger*
1 finely sliced raw carrot

2 T chopped sweet pickle
1 t vinegar
3 t brown sugar
2 t cornstarch
½ cup cold water

Fry ginger and pickles in the oil briefly. Mix cornstarch with water and combine with remaining ingredients, except for the carrots. Add this mixture to pickles and cook, stirring until the sauce thickens. Add carrots. Heat to boiling and serve. This sauce could also be added to Breakfast Carrots in place of water.

Try carrots sautéed and
   —curried with pineapple, banana, or poppy seeds.
   —glazed with lots of butter and some sweetening.
   —Other seasonings for carrots: allspice, caraway, cardamom, cinnamon, cloves, ginger, pepper, basil, mint, parsley, tarragon, thyme.

Onions

Onions! Magic beyond compare, onion goes with almost anything including watermelon: picks up tired dishes, sweetens greens, beefs up sauces, zests salads. But consider who is being served. Raw onion in particular does not suit everyone's taste.

The fleshy concentric layers of the onion are covered with a skin which is papery and inedible. Like potatoes, onions may be baked in their skins, but usually the onion is peeled prior to cooking or

eating. First the ends are trimmed off. Then the skin layers are slit, top to bottom, and peeled back around and off the onion. If one particular layer shares some fleshy part and some papery part, it is usually best to remove it entirely,

though some smaller skin patches may be removed separately. Now the onion is ready to be sectioned, sliced, diced, minced or grated.

Crying time. It'll help to peel all the onions first, then start cutting. Tear remedies include a wooden match between the teeth (okay to chew), chew on a piece of raw onion, put cut pieces in a covered bowl off to the side. Some people feel that onion skin is one vegetable trimming which is not especially good in stock.

Sliced Onions:

Cut the onion in half down its axis, then, placing half an onion flat side down, slice (or chop) parallel with the axis. When two-thirds of the section has been sliced, the remainder is tipped over and the slicing continues on the un-cut surface. The picture shows how the remainder of the onion half can be held for the last few cuts, balanced against the first finger and held in place with the thumb. The knife can be guided by the thumb knuckle. This is quite a useful grip to know in cutting many different vegetables, when it is often easier to turn the vegetable around before continuing to cut.

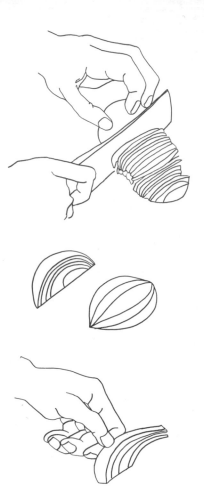

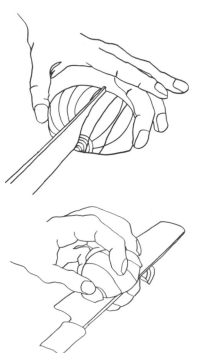

Dicing Onions:

Begin with the halved onion, placing the root end to the left. The root end should be left intact when cutting. Cut straight down and through, parallel with the axis and at appropriate intervals. Then make a couple of cuts with the knife parallel to the table top. Again leave the left end intact. Use a *gentle sawing* motion, so that the knife doesn't suddenly cut through to your fingers. Now cut straight down across all the

cuts you have made. Isn't it helpful to have pictures? Tip over the
intact part. Section it, turn
ninety degrees, and dice.

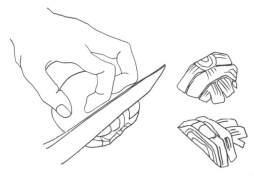

Minced onion: To start with,
dice the onion as finely as you can.
This gives a head start on the mincing,
described under Parsley.

Onions can take a lot of cooking, which brings out their sweetness
and "meatiness." Cooked onions lose their overwhelming sharpness,
and are quite compatible with other vegetables. Starting a mixed
vegetable sauté with onions seems to bring out all of the flavors
excellently.

Grated Onions

This is especially useful in salad dressings.

onion

Grate the onion or mince it finely. Use raw in sauce or salad dressing,
or sauté it lightly before using.

Sautéed Onions

onions   oil   salt

Slice, dice or section the onions. Sauté the onions from two to five
minutes. Allow longer cooking time for bigger onion sections. The
onions will first turn translucent, and then begin to brown. Onion
cooking may be completed in any of the following ways:
    —Steam five to ten minutes longer, seasoning with salt, pepper or
soy sauce.
    —Serve as an accompaniment or in a sauce.
    —Add one or two other vegetables and continue the sautéing for
two to three minutes before steaming to complete the cooking.
    —Add the sautéed onions to a simmering sauce or soup.
    —Add the sautéed onions to grain, bean, egg or cheese dishes.

Baked Onions

These come out very sweet and very mild, succulent.

onions

Bake the onions in their skins like potatoes. Thirty to forty minutes at 350°. Onions may also be skinned, then quartered or chunked, and baked in a small amount of water and/or oil.

Onion-Apple Stir-Fry

Which is sweeter? The apple's tartness blends well with the onion's sweetness.

onions   apples   raisins
vinegar or lemon juice   salt, pepper

Slice the onions and slice or chunk the apples. You can use about the same number of each. Sauté the onions until they are golden, about ten minutes. Add the apples and raisins, season mildly with the vinegar, cover, and steam until the apples have softened slightly. Season with salt and pepper. A bit of sugar can be used in place of the raisins.

Green Onion

Known variously as green onion, scallion, or spring onion, this is the long one with white root-end and slightly spreading green top. In most grocery stores these onions will be chopped down to twelve or fifteen inches, as the upper greens wilt. All of this onion is good—mild, yet zippy. The green as well as the white can be cut finely for salads, or in longer sections for cooking. Particularly when sliced diagonally, the green pieces make an excellent bright green alternative to parsley garnish. To prepare, first wash, then cut off roots and break off all wilted green stalks.

Slicing Green Onions

The pictures show how the onions are gripped by the left hand; thumb and last finger on the sides, then other fingers curled on top. The cut pictured is the most thorough way to cut green onions. Keeping the tip (or curve) of the knife on the table, the cut is made by pulling the knife down and toward you. The table-hugging tip cuts through all of the onion at some point, so that there is no chain of onion slices hung together where they were incompletely cut. Cutting on a long diagonal will make attractive

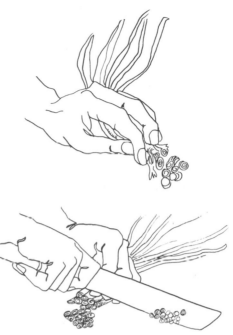

ellipses of green. Green onions can be used to decorate and season vegetables, grains, potatoes, eggs, cheese, soups, salads, main dishes, anything.

Leeks

Leeks, yet another form of onion, look like large scallions. Mild and sweet, they are frequently used in potato soups and *quiches*. We use the whole plant, prepared and sliced like scallions, but some cooks use just the white part.

Potato-Leek Soup

The sliced leeks are well-sautéed before being added to the rest of the dish.

3 parts finely sliced potatoes   2 parts sliced leeks or onion
milk or cream   seasonings   oil or butter

Sauté the leeks in oil for ten minutes. Add to the potatoes with enough hot water to cover. Simmer until well-cooked, about thirty minutes. Add cream or milk to desired thickness. Season with salt, pepper, garlic, mace if you like it. Serve hot or chilled. Cold potato soup with lots of diced cucumber is a good summer treat.

Leeks for Four

4-12 leeks, depending on size   butter   water   salt, pepper

Cut off leaves, leaving two inches of green. Trim roots. Cut in half lengthwise and wash. Melt the butter. Place the leeks flat side down and cook for a couple of minutes. Then add a cup of water, salt and pepper. Cover and simmer for ten minutes.

Garlic

Garlic is certainly a wonderful seasoning, for rounding out flavors—"suppressing the offensive flavors," as the Chinese would say, and supporting the appealing ones. Like the onion, to which it is related, garlic gets sweeter and loses much of its kick in long cooking. At home in the world of tomatoes and pasta, garlic also resides comfortably in the world of soy sauce. It is the standard pepper-upper for tired dishes, be they soups, sauces or casseroles, but a good cook will not over-rely on it.

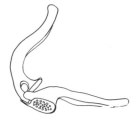

To use garlic, separate the cloves from the head. For most dishes, only one or two cloves will be needed. Some garlic presses are made for squeezing the cloves with the skin still on, but I like to peel it anyway. Rapping the cloves with the butt end of a knife or the flat of the blade will loosen the skin, and cutting or breaking off the ends of the clove will also facilitate its removal. If a garlic press is not available, mince the garlic as finely as possible, especially if you plan to use it raw.

Ginger Root

Ginger root is mentioned in several recipes. It is used much like garlic to enliven various dishes. It can be used by grating it on a fine grate, it can be sliced and minced, or it can be pressed in a garlic press.

Potatoes

Potatoes are marvelously soft, smooth, filling. Especially after a steady diet of brown rice, potatoes were always a treat: bland, earthy and pastey. Once I blew it by serving impenetrable baked potatoes—too bad.

We always eat potatoes with the skins—even mashed potatoes are good with flecks of skin. Scrub before cooking.

Cutting Potatoes

To cut potatoes into chunks, first
cut in half lengthwise. Place these
halves cut side down and cut them
lengthwise once or twice. Then
section the potato crosswise
into chunks.

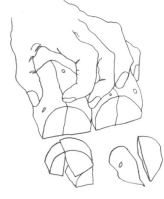

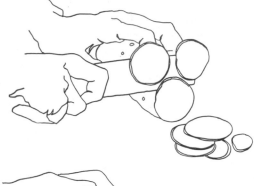

Cutting into Rounds:
Pictured here is an
example of the chop-
ping cut, down-and-
away-continuing
down-and-toward.

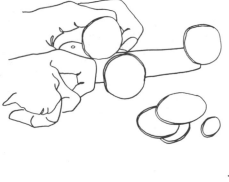

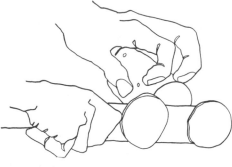

Yams & Sweet Potatoes

Even more than potatoes, yams and sweet potatoes are favorites of
ours. Deep yellow-orange with sweet, rich flavor, they can be cooked
in the same ways as potatoes, although the seasoning may vary. In
the recipes that follow, the names "yams" and "sweet potatoes" are
used interchangeably.

Home-Fried Potatoes

potatoes   oil   salt, pepper

Wash the potatoes and cut into thin slices, strips, or grate. Smaller pieces will cook more thoroughly and fry more quickly than larger ones. Use a generous amount of oil. Fry until the potatoes are brown and soft. Season. The pan can be covered so that the potatoes steam as well as fry. Open and turn the potatoes regularly.

Home-Fried Yams

sliced yams   oil   salt or soy sauce   (toasted sunflower seeds)

Fry these like the regular home fries. Once the yam slices are soft, add soy sauce and sprinkle generously with toasted sunflower seeds. For Onion Home Fries, fry the yams with sliced onions. May be served with yogurt.

Oven-Fried Potatoes

This is a good one to know about. These potatoes can come out well-browned without the fuss of French-frying.

potatoes   oil

Cut the potatoes in French-fry pieces. This can be done like carrot matchsticks, cutting the potato in half lengthwise first. Put the halved potato flat side down before cutting into strips, then sticks. Put the sticks on baking sheets, more or less one layer thick. Brush with oil and bake at 400° for about forty minutes. Baste several times. Sprinkle with salt.

Potato halves can be baked in the same way. Cut in half lengthwise. Place cut side up on baking sheet. Brush with oil, sprinkle with salt, bake. You may also put sliced or grated cheese on top for the last five minutes.

Steamed Potatoes & Vegetables

This can be cooked on top of the stove or in the oven.

potatoes   carrots   onions   water   oil   seasonings

Chunk all the vegetables. Put them in a saucepot or baking dish. Add a couple tablespoons of water and of oil. Sprinkle on salt and pepper, herbs. Cover and steam, or bake, for thirty minutes or so. May use winter squash in place of carrot.

Steamed Yams & Vegetables

yams   carrots   apples   (onion, winter squash)

This dish is made like the potatoes and vegetables above.

Just Yams & More

yams   water   salt

Scrub the yams, cut in halves or thirds crosswise. Then in quarters lengthwise. Arrange in a baking dish with a quarter inch of water on the bottom. Cover and bake until soft, about forty to sixty minutes.

   —Another method: Brush the yams with oil and bake, as in oven-fried potatoes.

   —*and more:* Bake the yams in a quarter inch of equal parts melted butter and orange juice. Baste several times.

Baked Potatoes

Wash the potatoes, dry them, rub on butter or oil. Bake at 350-400° for an hour or until fork-piercing tender. The bigger the potato the longer the baking time.

38

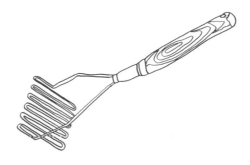

Mashed Potatoes

potatoes   milk, buttermilk, or sour cream   salt, pepper

Cut the potatoes in halves or thirds and cook them in lightly salted water until tender. Drain off the water and save it for soup. Mash the potatoes, mixing in the milk, buttermilk or sour cream. Season with salt and pepper. Do you like garlic? It's fantastic in mashed potatoes.

Variations:
    —Mix in grated cheese or sprinkle it on top.
    —Mix in cashew or walnut pieces. They'll blend right in with the skins.
    —Consider also sautéed mushrooms, parsley, green onion, diced and sautéed onion, celery, carrot, green pepper, cooked peas or corn kernels.

Mashed Yams

The ingredients can be layered in a casserole or mixed for immediate serving.

boiled or baked yams   butter   (grated orange rind)

Mash the yams with butter, salt and pepper. Mix in orange rind, cinnamon for seasoning. Serve.
    —Layer in casserole with diced onions and mushrooms, orange slices, banana slices. Dot the top with butter and bake up to half an hour at 350° to heat.
    —If the yams are mashed with *tahini* (sesame butter), sprinkle toasted sesame seeds on top.

Mashed Potatoes in the Skin

Bake the potatoes whole. Remove from oven when done. Cut in half lengthwise and scoop out the center, leaving the skin intact. Mash the potato you have removed, using one of the mashed potato recipes above, and then mound it back into the shells, maybe sprinkled with paprika, or grated cheddar. Pop them in the oven so they'll be hot when you want to serve them.

Yam Pie

Mash cooked yams and mix with sautéed onions. Season with salt or soy sauce, pepper, possibly mace or nutmeg. Spread into pie shell. (See p. 218.) Bake about thirty minutes. The top could be garnished with chopped nuts.

Yams on the Half-Shell

Mix mashed yams with orange juice, butter, orange rind, cinnamon and cloves. Mound this into scooped-out orange halves. Bake to heat.

Potato Salads

These can be dressed with mayonnaise or with an oil and vinegar dressing. The potatoes soak up the dressing if it is put on when they are still hot.

potatoes   choice of dressing
choice of vegetables and other ingredients: grated carrot,
sliced celery, hard-boiled egg, grated cheese, minced onion,
sliced green onion, parsley, black olives, pimento, dill pickle,
sliced radishes (keep it fairly simple)

Chunk the potatoes while they are still hot from being boiled. Mix in a liberal amount of dressing. Mustard, curry, tarragon, marjoram are possible additions to the standard oil-vinegar dressing. Chill the dressed potatoes. Prepare the other ingredients and mix them in also. Some of the optional ingredients can be saved for garnishing.

Sprouts

Sprouts can be started at any time of the year from beans, grains, and assorted seeds, including alfalfa, fenugreek, radish, mustard, sesame and sunflower. The little shoots are literally bursting with energy, as well as vitamins and protein. Crisp with moisture, they are also tender without having to be cut-up. Growing them at home, which isn't difficult, produces the freshest vegetable available.

Most easily sprouted are mung beans (which produce the well-known "Chinese bean sprout"), alfalfa and fenugreek seeds, and lentils. Oats, wheat and rye are fairly easy to grow, but their taste doesn't appeal to everyone. Soy beans can be sprouted if the non-sprouting beans are carefully sorted out as the sprouting progresses.

Sprouting seeds need to be kept in a dark, moist, warm environment. First soak the seeds overnight. Drain off the water and reserve it for some other cooking use. Then put the seeds into a wide-mouthed jar. Leave the end open, or cover it with cheesecloth or some other material which lets air in and out. Place the bottle on its side and keep it in a dark, warm place—in a cupboard or simply covered with a towel. To keep the seeds moist, rinse them once a day: cover the seeds with tepid water, swish the water gently around, then pour it through the cheesecloth or into a strainer. If the seeds are actually in water (after the initial soaking) they will tend to rot rather than sprout, so drain off the rinsing liquid thoroughly. Pictured are two jars of sprouts, inverted to drain.

Seeds can also be sprouted in a tray, plate, bowl or crock. Cover with a lid to keep moisture from evaporating. Pour the rinse water off through a strainer. Another method for sprouting is to put paper towels under and over the soaked seeds in the tray. Keep moist and out of the light. This method may take a little longer, but rinsing is not necessary.

Before eating, if the sprouts are put in the sunlight for several hours, they will turn green, which means that chlorophyl and vitamin C are present.

Seeds take from three to five days to sprout. Alfalfa sprouts are at the peak of their nutritional value when they are one inch long, but they can be eaten when they're several inches long, and even after the first leaves appear—"alfalfa lettuce."

Lentil sprouts peak at two inches, soy and mung bean sprouts at three inches.

Home-grown mung bean sprouts are darker than the commercial variety, which are chemically bleached.

For eating, grain sprouts are best when equal in length with the grain. Larger grain sprouts can be chopped or used in breads.

If the seeds don't sprout, it may be that the particular batch of seeds is old, defective or sprayed.

Sprouts are tasty and refreshing when eaten raw. They can be added to any salad, centered in a clump or tossed in with everything else. They also add a moist, light quality to sandwiches. Only bean sprouts are really suited to cooking. The others, being very delicate, can stand only brief cooking—add them at the end, or as a garnish for soups or mixed vegetable dishes.

Alfalfa Sprouts

Very popular in salads and sandwiches, these make an excellent side dish with beans as well. Lemon juice sweetened with honey dresses them adequately. For a more substantial side dish or salad how about:

Alfa-Banana Sprouts with Nuts

alfalfa sprouts   banana   walnuts

Mash the banana to make a dressing for the alfalfa sprouts. Thin and

42

season with lemon juice if necessary, then mix it with the sprouts and walnut pieces.

—Sliced apples and raisins could also be added to this dish.
—Fenugreek sprouts could be used in place of alfalfa sprouts.
—Other nuts or seeds could be used.

Stir-Fried Bean Sprouts

bean sprouts   celery   mushrooms   oil   salt   soy sauce

Slice the celery and the mushrooms. Stir-fry the celery for about two minutes before adding the mushrooms and sprouts. Stir to mix, add a couple tablespoons of water or stock and a tablespoon or so of soy sauce. Cover and steam two to three minutes. Adjust seasoning and serve.

Any number of other combinations are possible. Here are just a few:

—bean sprouts, onion and celery
—sprouts, peppers and carrots
—sprouts, asparagus and mushrooms
—These dishes could also be seasoned with grated fresh ginger (½ teaspoon) or garlic (one clove), a few pinches of sugar, a few drops of dark sesame oil. If more stock is added, it can be thickened with cornstarch dissolved in a small amount of cold water. A teaspoon of cornstarch will thicken a third of a cup of stock.

Bean Sprouts in Soup

Put them in for the last two minutes of cooking.

Lentil Sprouts

For a two month period several years ago the twenty mile dirt road into Tassajara was washed out. That provided quite an incentive to conserve food and to use things efficiently. Everything was at a premium. That's when we first started sprouting seeds. Two cups of lentils became over a gallon of sprouts. We had them almost every day for lunch, by themselves or mixed with wild greens: curly dock, miner's lettuce, chickweed, shepherd's purse. The dressing was vinegar and honey, except on occasion when a few lemons or oranges would show up. Living with some limitation like that, everything was delicious. Maybe with other things available lentil sprouts aren't quite that good, but I am still fond of them.

Lentil sprouts, somewhat heftier than mung bean sprouts, may require slightly longer cooking, but the same recipes can be followed. One combination to try is with onions and toasted sunflower seeds, seasoned with soy sauce and ginger.

Cabbage

Like any vegetable, cabbage is what you make it. Don't boil it down to mush and don't serve it with yucky sweet mayonnaise. Raw, it is best sliced quite thinly and given a little salt to start with. Cooked, it is good sautéed or lightly steamed. Raw cabbage has a natural peppery or slightly hot taste, which is vigorous and refreshing. Red cabbage is somewhat more pungent than green, and lends coloring to green salads or mixed vegetable dishes. Chinese cabbage (also known as *hakusai*, or *nappa*) has a very mild flavor and is quite juicy and tender.

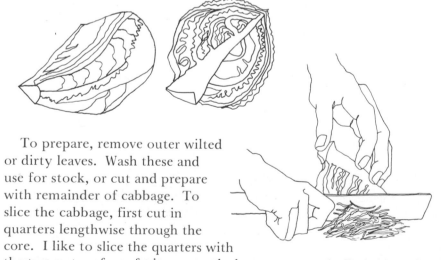

To prepare, remove outer wilted or dirty leaves. Wash these and use for stock, or cut and prepare with remainder of cabbage. To slice the cabbage, first cut in quarters lengthwise through the core. I like to slice the quarters with the two cut surfaces facing upwards, but some people find this awkward. Discover for yourself what works best for you. Cut parallel to to core or across the top in thin shreds for salads or sautéing, and in larger wedges for steaming or soups. The core, or cabbage heart, cut thinly, is also edible raw or cooked.

Thin Slice Salad

Can you cut the cabbage? As thin as you can without cutting yourself or taking forever. This is what makes the dish.

cabbage   salt

Cut the cabbage in thin slices. If you have some question about how to do this, see the preceding instructions for cutting. Sprinkle with salt and squeeze in your hands, this way and that, until some moisture begins to come out of the cabbage. If this isn't happening after a minute or two, add a little more salt and work it some more.

Thin Slice Salad with Orange & Green

cabbage   carrots   parsley   salt

Prepare the cabbage as in Thin Slice Salad. Wash the carrots and cut in one or two inch matchstick pieces. Mince the parsley finely. Add carrots and parsley to the cabbage and work them in. Add a bit more salt if necessary.

Thin Slice Salad Green & White

cabbage   celery   turnip   salt

The same as above, with celery cut in thin boomerang pieces and the turnip cut in small matchstick pieces.

Thin Slice Salad Galore

cabbage
other possibilities: red cabbage, chinese cabbage, celery,
spinach, chard, turnip, carrot, parsley, green onion, zucchini,
cucumber, asparagus, green bean, green pepper and other
vegetables that you can cut thinly;
plus sprouts which need not be sliced

Slice thinly. Salt lightly. Work with hands until juicy. Seasoning: thyme, basil, tarragon, marjoram; a bit of one or possibly two added to taste.

Instant Pickle

a thin slice salad   garlic   ginger   red pepper or tabasco sauce

Prepare a Thin Slice Salad. Add garlic to taste. Add ginger to taste. Easy-does-it red pepper or Tabasco sauce to taste. May be garnished with toasted sesame seeds.

Sautéed Cabbage

cabbage   oil   salt   small amount water

Cut the cabbage fairly thinly. Stir-fry a couple of minutes until cabbage wilts slightly. Add a couple of tablespoons of water, put on a lid and steam briefly.
    —with sunflower seed or sesame seed
    —with Parmesan cheese
    —with soy sauce, garlic, ginger, thickened with cornstarch

Sauterne Cabbage

I never liked cabbage until Ma cooked it with wine.

cabbage   oil   salt   sauterne

Prepare as in Sauteed Cabbage, adding the white wine in place of the water.

Tomato Sautéed Cabbage

cabbage   tomato   green onion or parsley   oil   salt

Again like Sauteed Cabbage. Section the tomatoes and slice green onions. After briefly stir-frying the cabbage, add onions and tomatoes, cover and cook just a couple of minutes, until the tomatoes are hot.

Red Cabbage & Apple

red cabbage   apples   brown sugar   vinegar   salt   pepper

Cut the cabbage in fairly large wedges. Slice the apples. Sauté the cabbage briefly before adding the apples. Then sprinkle on the brown sugar and cider vinegar to sweet and sour the taste. Salt and pepper lightly. Cover, cook for five minutes and serve.

This dish is often baked. Bake in covered baking dish for one half hour or more. It will be quite a bit limper than the unbaked version.

Steamed Cabbage

A rare bland delight.

cabbage

Cut the quartered cabbage in wide wedges. It is not necessary to separate the leaves. Place in steamer and cook for three to five minutes.

Steamed or sautéed cabbage can be served with lemon honey butter, seasoned with caraway seeds, garnished with roasted, chopped nuts.

Celery

Celery is notably stringy, crunchy, crisp, but it can also be tender luscious green with no strings attached. Used primarily as an accompaniment, celery attractively greens and compliments cauliflower, potatoes, squashes, soups, casseroles and salads. But like carrots and onions, celery can also be a main ingredient. Celery leaves are very much edible and, finely chopped like parsley, add seasoning. Especially in salads, celery is best when cut thinly, prettiest when cut in boomerang shape. (The thinner the celery is cut, the less string there is and the more easily chewed.)

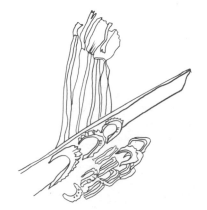

To prepare the celery, break off individual stalks and wash carefully, rubbing thumbs up and down the interior surfaces. With leaf end to the right, pick up main stalk and cut off side branches. Turn bottom end to right and trim off the end of stalks. For *boomerang pieces,* hold stalks on edge and cut on diagonal. For *comma pieces,* let stalks lie flat and cut on diagonal. For juicy, tender salad pieces, cut thinly on the diagonal. Celery is good in thin sliced cabbage salad.

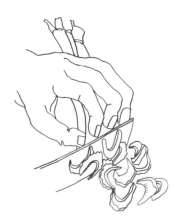

Orange Celery Salad

three stalks celery   two oranges (juice ½, pieces 1½)
one apple   salt

Wash celery and trim off leaves. Hold the stalks on edge and cut thin
pieces diagonally. Add salt lightly. Juice half of one orange. Peel
the rest and cut in rounds or half rounds. Wash and quarter the apple.
Cut out the seeds, and cut in slices. Mix all together. Need anything
else? Sprinkle chopped celery leaves on top.

Quick-Fry Celery

celery   oil   salt

Slice celery and stir-fry until tender. Sprinkle on some soy sauce if
you'd like.

Cream Cheese Celery

To make bigger pieces for this dish and still avoid stringiness, lay the
celery flat and cut on long diagonals. (The celery is not quite parallel
with the knife.)

5 stalks celery   oil   salt   2 oz. cream cheese
hot water   seasoning

Blend the cream cheese with ¼ cup hot water. Season with salt, pepper, herbs to taste. That's the sauce. Cook the celery as in quick fry
celery. Mix with sauce, or put celery in serving bowl and pour the
sauce over it.

Fancy Boiled Celery

celery   butter and cream or milk   salt and pepper

Cut celery in boomerangs. Boil in covered pot with just enough water
to cover celery. When tender, pour off most of the water for stock,
and add butter and cream, salt and pepper to taste.

Mushrooms

Mushrooms aren't really vegetables, of course, they're fungi. They like to grow from rot. I think most vegetarians must grow to love mushrooms, especially if they were meat-eaters previously, for mushrooms have a certain meaty quality. Dried mushrooms in particular have something of the chewiness of meat. The price per pound for mushrooms looks high, but there are a lot of mushrooms to a pound and, like garlic, a little can go a long way. A few mushrooms can be a good addition to almost any vegetable dish. I think I've had mushrooms with every vegetable except beets. Plus, there are mushroom sauces, mushroom soups, mushroom stuffings and mushrooms stuffed.

Mushroom lovers insist that mushrooms not be washed but, if anything, they only be wiped with a damp towel. Still, I prefer to give them a quick bath, lightly rubbing the tops with my thumbs.

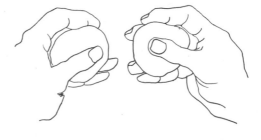

Mushrooms can be sliced on the large single blade of a grater, as well as with a knife as pictured. The chopping cut, down and slightly towards, is used

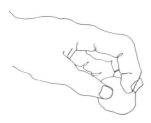

(shown in the picture). If the stems have darkened with age, they can be put in soup stock, or chopped and sautéed, then added to other dishes.

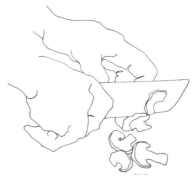

50

Mushrooms don't require much cooking. They brown in just three to four minutes and steam to perfection in five minutes. When added to soups at the last minute they bob handsomely on the surface. Mixed into potato dishes, grain dishes, stuffings, casseroles, mushrooms can stand a more lengthy cooking.

Raw Mushrooms in Salads

Raw mushrooms for lettuce, cabbage or other salads can be sliced or quartered. Slicing them creates beautiful looking pieces, while quartered mushrooms add a fine chewiness.

Sautéed Mushrooms

mushrooms   oil (butter)   salt

Slice or quarter mushrooms. Cook in butter or oil, three to four minutes. Season with salt and pepper. Sprinkle with parsley, cress or green onion. For further variation add some roasted, chopped nuts, or mix in some sour cream and heat gently. Smaller amounts of sautéed mushrooms can be used to garnish other vegetable dishes, and can be added to grain, bread cube or potato stuffings.

Sautéed Mushrooms with Sherry

After sautéing the mushrooms for two minutes in a generous amount of butter or oil, sprinkle on a few spoonfuls of flour. Stir this in and continue frying for a couple of minutes. Douse liberally with sherry so that a sauce, but not a soup, results. Simmer for about two more minutes.

Sautéed Mushrooms & Onions

Onions and mushrooms are an excellent accompaniment for other vegetables, grains, eggs. Sauté the onion for a couple of minutes before adding the mushroom as above. This is good with bean sprouts.

Marinated Onion & Mushroom

onion   mushrooms   vinegar-sugar-sherry   or sake-soy sauce

For this one, leave the mushrooms whole or in large sections. Add the marinade to the sauteed onions and mushrooms and simmer for a few minutes. Remove and let cool. Note that this dish can be served hot if the marinade is thickened with cornstarch dissolved in cold water. (1T cornstarch and 1T cold water for every cup of marinade.

Mushroom Sauce

Add briefly sautéed mushroom slices to the White Sauce (p. 196).

Mushroom Soup

Use hot milk to thin the White Sauce with Mushrooms to soup consistency.

About Dried Mushrooms:

I have found dried mushrooms available at Italian groceries and at Oriental food shops. There are basically two different varieties, but both are prepared in the same way. The Oriental kind are smaller and require about thirty minutes of soaking in warm water. The European ones, if in strips, are soaked for about the same length of time; if they are whole it will take up to two or three hours of soaking in order to soften them.

Be sure to save the water in which the mushrooms were soaked. There will be some dirt at the bottom of the soaking bowl, so after removing the mushrooms, carefully pour off the liquid or strain it through a paper towel. This soaking liquid will be a flavorful addition in the dried mushroom dish itself, or in some other soup, sauce, grain or casserole dish. After soaking, the mushrooms can be used whole or sliced. The Oriental type can be cooked in ten minutes, while the European type takes twenty minutes or more. If nothing

else, simmer them in the soaking liquid or a sauce. Then they are
ready to serve or to add to another dish.

A Dried Mushroom Sauce

This can be served with many dishes, for instance greens, asparagus,
snow peas, broccoli, onion, eggplant, green beans, carrots, or some
combination of these.

10-12 dried mushrooms (Oriental)　　green onion　　grated ginger
water for soaking　　1 T cornstarch, dissolved in 1 T cold water
salt　　sugar　　soy sauce　　sherry or sake

Soak the mushrooms and reserve the soaking liquid as described above.
Season a cup of this liquid with salt, then soy sauce, wine and sugar.
If using them, grate the ginger (a half teaspoon or so) and section the
green onions (3 or so). Stir fry the mushrooms for two minutes, then
an additional two minutes with the green onion and ginger. Mix in
the seasoned liquid, heat quickly, then simmer gently for ten minutes.
With the mixture bubbling, briskly mix in the cornstarch which has
been dissolved in the cold water. *Note:* the stock can also be seasoned
with just sugar and soy sauce.

Parsley

Parsley can be used as an ingredient, a seasoning or a garnish. It is
excellent in soups, especially those which seem overly sweet, like onion, carrot, or yam, and in those which may be too tart or too bland.
Parsley sprigs are a famed and overused garnish. Green onion, water
cress, green pepper, celery, cucumber and alfalfa sprouts, artfully
sliced and arranged, could all be considered as alternatives.

Mincing

The parsley, or whatever vegetable is to be minced, is first cut as finely as possible. With parsley, several sprigs are bunched together and then cut finely crosswise. The finely cut pieces are piled up to be minced. If a curving chef's knife is used, the knife is rocked up and down through the pile. The top edge of the blade is tilted in the direction in which the knife is travelling. Each chop is further and further away, or closer and closer, to the chopper. At intervals the dispersed pile is regrouped for further mincing. If a straight edged Japanese vegetable knife is used, the tip can be held down or not as you prefer.

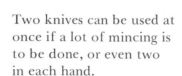

Two knives can be used at once if a lot of mincing is to be done, or even two in each hand.

54

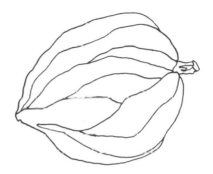

Winter Squash

Winter squashes are harvested in the fall and, if their tough outer skin is intact, they will keep for several months over the winter. They include Banana Squash, Hubbard, Acorn ... even pumpkin, which makes heart-warming soup and vegetable dishes as well as pie. Smooth, squashy and among the most satisfying of wintertime foods, when cooked these vegetables are like a piece of summer sunshine. They are usually steamed or baked, or a combination of both. If the skin is tough, the squash can be eaten by scooping out the pulp with a spoon. Thinner skins can be eaten.

Steamed Winter Squash

squash   salt   water

Put about half an inch of water in the bottom of a pan. If practical, the squash can go in whole. Or cut it open, remove the seeds and cut into serving-size chunks before putting in the water. Sprinkle on some salt, heat to boiling, then turn down to simmer. Put on a lid and let cook until tender, about thirty to forty minutes.

Baked-Steamed Winter Squash

squash   salt   water

This is the same as above, only put the squash in an oven pan instead of a saucepan. A little water on the bottom, a cover on the top (or aluminum foil), and bake it in a 350° oven for fifty to sixty minutes.

Baked Winter Squash

squash   oil (butter or margarine)

Cut up the squash, remove seeds and arrange the pieces in a baking dish. Baste the pieces generously with oil or melted butter, and bake in a 350° oven from forty to sixty minutes, depending on the size of the pieces. Baste every ten or fifteen minutes for added moistness and flavor.

This recipe can be made with whole squashes. Baste with oil and bake until knife or fork-tender. May be carved at the table like a roast.

Basting variations:
—equal parts of oil and orange juice
—two parts oil, one part lemon juice, sugar or honey to taste
—a few dashes cinnamon, nutmeg or allspice in any of the basting mixtures

Pumpkin Soup

pumpkin   onion   salt   oil   water
croutons   cinnamon, nutmeg

Cut the pumpkin open and remove seeds and the stringy portion of the interior. Cut the pumpkin into about one inch cubes. Slice the onion, and sauté for a couple of minutes, then add the pumpkin. Sauté for about five minutes, stirring, and then add a cup of water, put on a lid, and let it simmer for forty to fifty minutes, until the pumpkin is quite tender. At this point the pumpkin, or some portion of it, can be mashed to thicken the broth. Add some more water to the onion-pumpkin mixture to make it soupy. Heat and season with salt, cinnamon, and nutmeg. The soup may be garnished with croutons.

Other Winter Squash Soups

winter squash (hubbard, acorn, banana)   onion   salt   oil
water   cinnamon, nutmeg   croutons   (tomato paste)

This soup is made like the pumpkin soup above, unless there is some
doubt whether or not the skin of the squash will be soft enough to
eat after it's cooked. Cooked pumpkin skin is thin enough to eat and
the skin of the Acorn Squash and Banana Squash usually will be too,
but Hubbard Squash and some of the others may have quite tough
skin, up to an eighth of an inch thick. In this case, the skin can be
easily removed after cooking. Cut the squash in larger pieces, three
or four inches square, and after these have cooked in a small amount
of water until tender, let them cool a bit and then remove the skins
by scraping away the pulp. Cut up or mash this as you will, return
it to the cooking liquid, and add some more water. Season with salt,
cinnamon, nutmeg and possibly tomato paste if it's handy. Serve
with croutons.

Cool Weather

Beets

Beets are red, and once cut open or cooked, beets will tint everything which comes into contact with them—hands, knife, cutting
board, egg whites and potatoes turn pink, and even celery and carrots will redden with prolonged contact, a wondrous effect.

Not just red, beets have a sweet, earthy flavor, solid and rich.
It is cooking which brings out the sweetness. Raw beets are very
occasionally eaten grated in salad. They taste, quite simply, like
dirt, which may not be so bad, but the more usual way is to cook
them first and then grate. Beet greens, including the red stems, are
quite edible, tender and mild tasting. They can be cooked with the
beets or separately as a greens dish. The cooking time for beets
depends on the size of the beets and so will be shorter if the beets
are cut up first. Beets are one of the few vegetables that can stand
being cooked past tenderness and still retain much of their delicate
flavor. Two pounds of beets without tops for four servings.

Boiled Beets

This is the usual first step in cooking beets, after which any number
of things can be done, if need be or fancy is free. Beets have a skin
or peel which, if not cut at the stem or root, will hold in most of the
juices during cooking, so scrub the beets as best you can with the

root and about one inch of stem attached. The beets are covered or half-covered with salted water, then covered with a lid and simmered until fork-piercing tender. One-half to one hour for smaller beets, up to two hours for larger ones. With a pressure cooker, use just an inch of water and cook twelve to eighteen minutes, depending on size.

When drained and cool enough to handle, one of the most sensuous pleasures in cooking awaits: slipping off the skins. A gentle tug dislodges the stems, then, squeezing the beet proper, out pops the bright interior— smooth, slippery, warm and plump in your very hand.

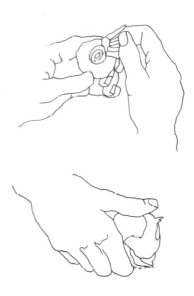

Next, slice or chunk the beets. I like to do it so that each piece retains some of the roundness of the whole beet—for example, cutting the beet in half and, laying the pieces flat side down, slicing them into half rounds. Or perhaps cutting the whole beet into eighths.

Then, reheat the cut beets with a bit of butter, salt and pepper. Beyond this you might:

—*dress* lightly with vinegar or lemon juice

—*season* with cinnamon and cloves, with garlic or with ginger

—*garnish* with minced parsley, thinly sliced green onion, water cress or perhaps with grated cheese, Parmesan or Jack.

Sautéed Beets

Beets can also be sautéed. Cut off the roots and stems. Scrub the beet. The skin is edible, so don't worry about peeling it off. Cut the beet in slices or small chunks. Sauté for five minutes, then add a little liquid, cover and steam for another five to ten minutes. Any of the seasoning ideas already mentioned could be incorporated into this dish. Other vegetables could be used in combination with the beets, such as onion, cabbage, greens, carrots.

Beets & Greens

cooked beets   beet greens

Boil and cut beets as in basic recipe. Cut the greens and stems into one inch sections crosswise. When reheating prepared beets, add the greens, cover and steam for a couple of minutes. Then stir the beets and greens together, adjust the seasoning, and continue cooking until done—another two or three minutes.

Beets with Sour Cream

This is an old standard, sweet and sour.

beets (with or without greens)
sour cream (or yogurt, or cream cheese thinned with buttermilk)

Add sauce when reheating beets or when greens are stirred in. Minced onion, horseradish and chives are all good in this dish.

Baked Beets

Any of the alternatives above are good with these, too.

beets

Prepare the beets as for boiling, leaving on the root and an inch of stem. Bake at 350° for one half to one hour. Let cool slightly, remove skins and serve.

Beet Greens

Aside from cooking for a few minutes with the beet roots, these may be prepared like other greens.

Radishes

Radishes have a snappy, peppery flavor which is similar to that of turnips. Aside from being served whole as an appetizer, radishes can be sliced and added to almost any salad: lettuce, cabbage, potato, bean, vegetable, corn. Some people find it is easier to leave the stem and leaves attached when slicing so there is something to hold on to.

Shown is the chopping cut made down and slightly toward. Radishes can also be cooked like turnips or carrots, only they take less time. Radish slices provide an excellent garnish for many

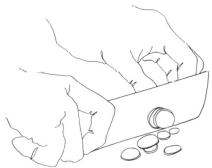

soups, added just a minute or so before serving. The white radish, known as icicle radish or *daikon*, has a hot taste, so it may be quite a hit in salads, or again it can be cooked like carrots.

Radish Salad

> radishes, sliced   green pepper, slivered   carrot, grated
> vinegar   soy sauce   honey or sugar

Sweeten the vinegar to taste and season with soy sauce. Mix with the vegetables.

61

Radish-Raisin Salad

This salad uses some of the radish greens as well as the radishes.

a dozen radishes
3-4 radish tops
1/3 carrot
a dozen lettuce leaves

¼ cup raisins
oil
vinegar
soy sauce

The radish greens are somewhat tough, so try to cut them thinly.
Salt and press them while the rest of the salad is being prepared (p. 12).
Slice the radishes in rounds. Cut the carrot into short matchstick
pieces. Tear or cut the lettuce into small pieces. Mix up the dressing—about equal parts oil, vinegar, soy sauce. Toss everything
together.

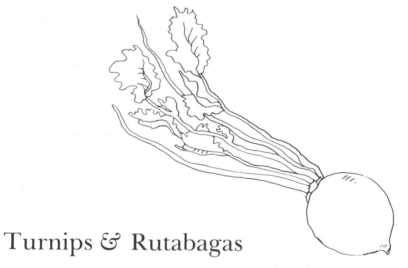

Turnips & Rutabagas

Is it ruta-baa-ga's or ruta-bay-ga's? They're good either way. These
are of course both root vegetables: the turnip round and white, often
with a purplish area on its skin; the rutabaga more oval shaped and
orange-brown. When eaten raw they have, as radishes have, something
of a peppery, zesty taste. When cooked just to tenderness, their taste
is clean, mild, with a slight bite. Cooking to mushiness will draw out
the most odorous and penetrating flavors, which is okay, but like
well-cooked cabbage, not a taste everyone acquires. Here are several
ways to use them.

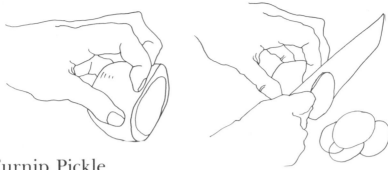

Turnip Pickle

This is a Japanese-style pickle, originally made with seaweed.

turnips   salt   lemon peel and juice
sugar or honey   kombu seaweed (may be omitted)

Here's another recipe which tests how well you're cutting. Wash the turnip and trim off the root and the green at the top. Cut the turnip in rounds as thin as you possibly can. Half rounds won't have the same wholeness, but they'll do, too. Put the slices in a bowl with about a half teaspoon of salt for each medium sized turnip, and salt under pressure (p. 12) for half an hour or more. (It can even be overnight.) Meanwhile, peel a lemon with a vegetable peeler and cut the strips of peel into quarter inch squares. Soak the *kombu* for twenty minutes and cut it in quarter inch squares also. If there is a lot of water with the turnips after salting, pour it off and save it for soup stock. Mix the lemon juice with sugar or honey to taste and then toss everything together. The turnip is good after just the salt and the pressing, too.

Turnip or Rutabaga Stir-Fry

A natural for those little-ish turnips which come with a lot of green.

turnips   turnip greens   oil   salt   pepper

Wash the turnips, then cut in half and slice. Wash the greens, cut in one inch sections and keep separate from the turnips. Stir-fry the turnips for three or four minutes. Turn the heat down to medium low, put in the greens and put on a lid. Let it cook for four or five minutes. Check it once in the meantime. Is it doing okay? Temperature alright? Turnips not quite tender?

With or without the greens, grated cheddar cheese may be sprinkled on top just before serving.

—Carrots, turnips and greens are good together. Start the stir-frying with the carrots for a couple of minutes, then continue as above.

—Or how about onion and celery with rutabaga? Begin the stir-frying with the onion, then the celery briefly, then as above.

—For *Baku-Rei Garden Thinnings Hot Salad:* Use all those small root-crop thinnings, plus edible greens. Stir-fry in (olive) oil. After the greens have begun to wilt, season the dish with vinegar, salt and pepper. Steam another minute or two. Also good with onion and toasted sesame seed.

Roasted Turnips or Rutabagas

turnips and/or rutabagas   oil or butter

Wash the vegetables, dry, and brush with oil or melted butter. Place on baking sheet or pan and bake for about thirty minutes at 350°. May be garnished with grated cheese and/or chopped parsley when serving.

Turnip or Rutabaga Bake

turnip (rutabaga)   (onion, carrot)
white or brown sauce (see Sauces)

Wash turnip and cut in quarters, sixths or eighths. If using them, cut onion and carrot in good-sizes chunks. Make up the sauce. Put the heated sauce and vegetables in a greased baking dish and bake at 350° for twenty-five to thirty minutes.

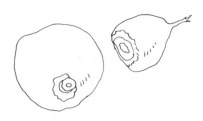

Greens

This is mainly about chard and spinach, probably the two commonest greens, but what is said can be applied to most cooking greens. Beet greens (one of the most tender), turnip greens, collard and mustard greens, kale (probably the toughest green) and *bok choy* all are often available. Of these, only spinach is really appetizing when eaten raw. Most of the others are slightly bitter or tart, but other flavors can be brought out depending on the way they are prepared.

Greens cook down by quite a lot, so to come out with the same cooked volume as with other vegetables, it is necessary to start with three to four times as much raw volume. We have found, however, that people eat about the same amount of greens as they would of other vegetables.

When doing a combination vegetable dish with greens, the other vegetables can be stir-fried in a frying pan and then transferred to a larger pot. Then there is plenty of room to add the greens on top of the other vegetables for steaming.

Chard and Spinach

Spinach greens add a tender meatiness to salads, while chard is tougher and tends to pucker the mouth when eaten raw. Spinach leaves have thin, easy-chewing stems, while chard leaves are centered on a broad, stringy white stalk. There is also a spectacularly beautiful chard with leaves centered on a red stalk with red ribs extending out into the green leafiness. If prepared by themselves, these greens are probably best steamed, but they can also be sautéed or briefly boiled. Often slightly bitter, all greens can be sweetened when cooked in combination with onions, carrots, bananas or such, and can be a main dish when cooked with eggs.

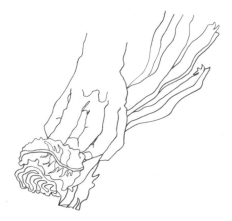

Spinach Salad

For salads, spinach can be rolled up and sliced very thinly, or it can be torn into fairly small pieces with the stems sliced. Spinach can be used in combination with other salad greens. When used alone, it may want a creamy dressing, some chopped hard-boiled egg, or maybe some grated cheese. Minced onion is good, too, if you and your guests think so. Grated carrot and lemon juice is another alternative. Little chunks of tomato make a bright addition.

Whole Steamed Spinach

Spinach is particularly elegant and tasty cooked this way. The funny thing is that most people don't know what it is. I have heard people commenting, "Oh my, how gorgeous—what is it?" One time someone said, "I think maybe it's dandelion leaves." For such a simple dish the reactions are often astounding. What makes the dish is some careful attention to details.

spinach   salt   melted butter or margarine   lemon wedges

Wash the spinach and as you do so, make an effort to keep all of the stems going in the same direction. Arrange the spinach in the steamer, again in piles of leaves with stems in the same direction. Sprinkle in a little salt, picking up piles of leaves here and there. Steam the spinach a bare two to four minutes. Arrange attractively with lemon wedges (an extra star if you've taken the seeds out) on a heated serving platter. Spoon some melted butter over the spinach. Serve immediately.

Steamed Spinach Salad

spinach

Steam a scant two or three minutes. Chill. Sprinkle on a little oil or lemon juice or soy sauce, or mix with a regular dressing. Can also be served with grated, cooked beets and lightly steamed cauliflower.

Steaming Other Greens

For most other greens, the stems or stalks will take longer to cook than the leafy part. So, if the greens are cut crosswise into one inch sections, the pieces of stems or stalks can be steamed for three minutes before adding the leafy parts.

Green, Orange & Onion

Once again, steamed greens—only on a bed of carrot and onion.

greens   an onion   a carrot   oil   salt

Wash the greens and cut them in one or two inch sections. Slice the onion and cut the carrot into small pieces. Sauté the onion for a minute, then add stalk pieces and the carrot, continuing to sauté for three to five minutes. Turn the heat down and add the greens, or as much as will fit comfortably. Cover and let steam for a minute, then open, fold in the greens, adding the rest if they didn't fit at first. Steam another two or three minutes.

Green, Orange & Mushroom

This time carrot and mushroom round out the greens.

greens   a carrot   some mushrooms (a half dozen?)   oil   salt

Sauté the carrots first for three to five minutes and then add the mushrooms, for another minute. Finally, the greens as before.

Spinach Goes Bananas with Sesame

spinach or other greens   a banana or two
toasted sesame seeds or other nuts/seeds

Wash and section the greens. Slice the banana and toast the sesame seeds. Stir-fry the greens, turning them over while adding more greens until all are in the pan. Check the seasoning, add the bananas, put on a lid and wait just long enough for the bananas to get hot. Sprinkle with toasted sesame seeds, or would you prefer chopped, roasted hazel nuts?

Spinach Could Also Go Apricot

The food trippers are tearing their hair, "How could you?" and licking their lips, "We love you." Oh me, oh my.

greens   apricots

Somehow the sesame doesn't seem quite as appealing in this one. Make it like Spinach Going Bananas. Cut the apricots in quarters or sixths. Stewed dried apricots or canned apricots could also be used.

Greens Get Egged On

The egg can appear or disappear, but in any case the greens are meaty.

greens   oil   salt, pepper   eggs

Sauté-steam the greens until they're nearly done. Stir in some beaten egg or eggs. With few eggs and lots of stirring, the eggs will blend in much like a seasoning. With more eggs and less stirring, the effect will be more omelette-like. A few teaspoons of soy sauce can go in with the eggs. If you like onions, start by sautéing the yellow kind, or sprinkle on some chopped green onion as garnish.

Greens Go Nuts

Just like they go bananas. Reputed to be a good protein combination, as well as being delicious. You may try almonds, walnuts, peanuts, filberts, etc., and also sunflower or sesame seeds.

Some Other Green Ideas

Spinach: onion, lemon juice, nutmeg, salt and pepper.
Mustard greens: cook five minutes first, then cook with mushrooms for five. Garnish with egg slices.
Dandelion leaves: olive oil, garlic: brown garlic one minute, then sauté-steam greens and mushrooms five.

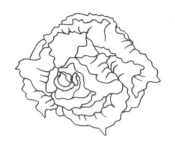

Lettuce

Head, Romaine, Boston, Oak Leaf, Red Leaf, Butter

Lettuce includes a wide variety of tender, leafy greens. Head lettuce and romaine are two with crispy-crunchy leaves, while the others tend to have softer, more velvety leaves. There are many exacting prescriptions for turning lettuce into salad. What follows is a general idea.

The idea is that somebody is going to eat some lettuce. Why not just rinse off the earth and serve it? If you appreciate and enjoy lettuce like this and the other people eating do also, read no further, nothing could be simpler. But maybe a little salt is added to bring out its natural taste. What happens when salt is added is that water is drawn out of the lettuce. It goes limp, loses its crisp. With cabbage this is appropriate, but lettuce leaves, more delicate than cabbage, don't have crisp to spare. The answer to this is get the lettuce coated with oil first. The salt won't penetrate nearly as fast. But now the lettuce is sure gummed up with oil. What cuts oil is vinegar. A bit of zing, too, not bad. So that's the basic dressing: oil, vinegar and salt. Beyond this basic dressing we can explore ways to further amplify, mollify, pacify. More about that in the Salad section. For now let's take care of the lettuce.

Focus some attention and energy on the activity and there is no longer time or resolve to mutter about how tedious it is.

Washing and drying lettuce: Dirt is one of the most unappetizing things that could garnish lettuce. It adds a lot of hesitation and reluctance to chewing. It may be that only the outer leaves of the

70

head of lettuce need washing. These leaves will often have some dirt tucked away in their folds or at the base of their stalks. It is often recommended to wash each leaf individually under running water, since soaking leeches flavor and nutrients out of the lettuce. This is fairly impractical in large scale cooking. To conserve time and water, several leaves at a time are placed in water. Take a floating leaf in each hand, and while rubbing the inside of the stalks with the thumbs, swish them around in the water. Remove from the water, give them a quick shake and place in a colander or strainer for further draining. Wash the entire bunch of leaves first, then take the lettuce from the colander, shake off water, tear into smaller pieces or cut with a stainless steel knife, which won't react with the lettuce.

Wet lettuce will water down the dressing, and the oil will not stick to the leaves, so it must be dried. The most practical way is by twirling it. A homemade cheesecloth sack works best, but we've also used a dish towel or a used onion bag. The lettuce goes into the bag and is swung briskly in an arc so that the water flies off. Keep the dried lettuce in the refrigerator, covered with a damp towel. The lettuce will be even crisper if you can fit it in the freezer for half an hour or so—not so long that it actually freezes.

Here are some alternatives for dressing a salad:

Two-Step Salad Toss

A simple way to dress a salad on a day to day basis.

> *olive or other salad oil   vinegar or lemon juice*
> *salt, pepper   (herbs)*

First toss the salad with oil. Start with a tablespoon or two, toss well, and see that each leaf has got some. When sufficiently oiled, sprinkle on the vinegar and lemon juice, salt, freshly ground pepper, and perhaps dust with herbs, all just to your taste. Toss well. Done properly, there won't be a puddle of dressing on the bottom of the salad bowl or plate, and the dressing will give a little kick without being overpowering. A further refinement is to keep cloves of garlic in the salad oil and marinate herbs in the vinegar.

71

Oriental Dressing

Soy sauce is excellent when used in place of the salt. For Oriental dressing use rice wine vinegar, a couple drops of dark sesame oil, along with the soy.

Lemonade Lettuce

This makes a light, refreshing, plain tasting salad. Maybe a bit strange at first, but the sweetened, fragrant lemon leads right into some honest lettuce.

lemon juice   honey

Sweeten the lemon juice to taste. Mix thoroughly. Dip a piece of lettuce in it to sample. This is a wonderful dressing for wild, edible greens such as miner's lettuce, chick weed, shepherd's purse and curly dock. It can also be made with vinegar and sugar.

Dairy Dressing

Start with a dairy product and fiddle. Hopefully this is another simple and enjoyable way to dress a salad.

sour cream	*oil*
buttermilk	*vinegar or lemon juice*
cottage cheese	*garlic*
ricotta cheese	*salt, pepper*
cream cheese	*herbs*
yogurt	*dry mustard*

Use one or more of the dairy products. For instance, if using cream cheese, you may want to soften it up and thin it out with buttermilk. Add vinegar to taste, starting with just a spoonful or two. Add the oil for consistency and clinginess. Then salt, pepper, garlic, herbs and so forth to taste. It needn't be too fancy. Some sugar or honey may also be added.

Nut-Butter Dressing

nut butter   oil   vinegar
salt or soy sauce   pepper

Make this like Dairy Dressing.

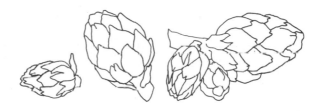

Artichokes

Artichokes are one of the most spectacular and aristocratic of vegetables, despite (or maybe because of) the fact that most of it is thrown away. A thistle, they are grown in California in an area centering around Castroville, the "Artichoke Capital of the World." Artichokes are served either whole, or if they are small the outer leaves can be removed and the inner portion served as an "artichoke heart." Whole artichokes are usually boiled or steamed, while the hearts can also be sautéed, deep-fried or pickled for salads. Artichokes are not eaten raw, but may be served either hot or cold.

To wash artichokes, hold them by the stem and swish them briskly up and down in water. Some of the tougher outer leaves may be removed. Cut off the stem flush with the lower leaves. The artichokes can be cooked like this or the top one-quarter to one-third of the leaves may be cut off with knife or scissors. The stem, when peeled, may be cooked and eaten along with the rest.

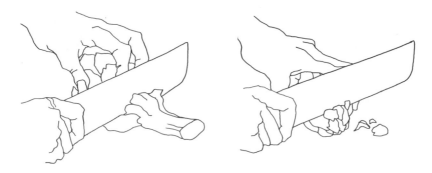

73

Steamed or Boiled Artichokes

This is the way artichokes are usually prepared. They'd be pretty tough to cut up and fry, though baking is a possibility. Slip the washed and trimmed artichokes into the boiling salted water or arrange in a steamer. If cooking in the liquid, cover, bring the water to a boil and then turn down the heat. Simmer for forty minutes, or until the outer leaves may be easily removed. If steaming, the artichokes will probably take from forty minutes to an hour to cook. Check periodically to make sure that there is still water in the lower part of the steamer.

Optionals: Want to dress up the artichokes? One of the easiest things to do is to cut off the upper portion of the leaves so that the  tops of the artichokes are basically level. Loosen and spread the leaves apart, then sprinkle herbs between the layers. Use sweet basil, tarragon, thyme or possibly marjoram or oregano. One herb fragrance will penetrate quite well. Another alternative is to season the cooking liquid. For this add the juice of a lemon, some onion and/or garlic, some celery, a part of a bay leaf and any other seasoning that you're fond of.

When eating artichokes hot, dip the petals in melted butter or mayonnaise on their way to your mouth, or take a look at the other suggestions in the Asparagus section.

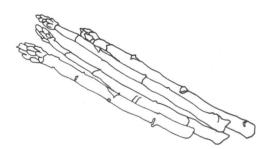

Asparagus

Fresh asparagus is a wonderful treat, available for only a short time in the late spring, when the new shoots of the asparagus plant are harvested. The cut end of the shoots may be set in water to help maintain freshness. This end is frequently white and tough to chew. It can be removed by gripping it as close to the end as possible and

74

snapping it off. The shoot will break right at the tender eating mark. The asparagus is now ready to be eaten raw or cooked whole, boiled  or steamed, or to be cut up for sautéing. Cook asparagus only until tender. Anything short of this is tasty too, juicy with a slight crunch. Hot or cold, asparagus is usually served with mayonnaise, but there are many other possibilities.

Asparagus in Salads

Asparagus makes a succulent, almost meaty addition to salads. It may be simply sliced raw, or it can be briefly boiled or steamed and then cut into salad pieces.

Basic Asparagus

asparagus

Prepare the asparagus as above. Place in boiling salted water and when the water returns to boiling, turn the heat down so that the asparagus simmers. If the asparagus is to be served cold, some crispness is especially appetizing, so cook the asparagus anywhere from two to eight minutes, depending on how much crispness you want. To cool, spread out the asparagus on a large plate. Hot boiled or steamed asparagus is good with melted butter, lemon juice or maybe **Cream Cheese Sauce** (see Sauces). For cold asparagus dips, try one of these:

Asparagus with Lemon Mayonnaise

To prepare the mayonnaise, add lemon juice to taste. This makes an amazing difference in the mayonnaise. One attractive serving arrangement is to put the mayonnaise at one end of a platter, then arrange the asparagus to be swimming towards it.

Asparagus with Cream Cheese or What You Will

Mayonnaise isn't the only thing to dip asparagus in.

asparagus   cream cheese   sour cream or milk or yogurt   lemon?

Cook the asparagus as in the preceeding recipe. Soften the cream
cheese by working it with a spoon or fork, and thin it to mayonnaise
consistency by adding sour cream, milk or yogurt a little bit at a time.
If you like lemon, add some juice. Salt and pepper are also permitted.
Starting with yogurt or sour cream is alright too. In any case, herbs
can be utilized, although it is not always possible to top the preceeding masterpiece by adding something else. For starters, you can try
a bit of sweet basil or tarragon, marjoram or oregano, thyme or dill.
Chopped parsley or watercress?

Asparagus with Guacamole

Deep green and light green blending.

asparagus   guacamole

Cook the asparagus as in the basic recipe, and serve with a guacamole
dip (see Avocado).

Basic Asparagus Over Easy

Asparagus can be cut on the diagonal for sautéing. First it's cut.
Then it's sautéed.

*some asparagus   one small yellow onion
one carrot   oil   salt*

Prepare the asparagus. Then cut in oval shaped pieces, leaving the
buds intact at the tender tip end. Asparagus may also be cut with
the Chinese rolling cut. Slice or dice the onion and cut the carrot in
ovals, rolling cut, half-rounds or what-have-you. Sauté the onion for
about a minute. Add the carrot and fry this with the onion for a

76

minute or two. Then add the asparagus. Toss with the onion and carrot for a minute, then add a couple tablespoons of water, put a lid on, turning the heat down to medium or medium low. Cook for two to five minutes until tender. (The smaller the pieces, the shorter the cooking time.)

Variations: Asparagus over easy and fancy
  —*With mushrooms:* Prepare everything as in the recipe above. Add mushrooms for the last three minutes of cooking.
  —*With cheese:* Sprinkle some cheese on top of the asparagus when it's in the serving bowl. Try onion, asparagus and cheddar cheese. Or carrot, asparagus and Jack cheese. Even onion, carrot, asparagus, mushroom and Parmesan. Whatever you have or like or needs using.
  —*With nuts:* This is of course your basic asparagus over easy with nuts. You can figure it out.

Broccoli

Another of cabbage's many cousins, broccoli makes green, succulent eating. The broccoli flowerettes extend from a thick main stalk. Both the flowerettes and the stalk are edible, but the outside of the main stalk is generally tough and stringy. If this stalk is cut into eighth or quarter inch rounds, the stringiness is not so noticeable. Or the tougher outside layer of the stalk can be peeled off. Beginning at the bottom of the stalk, slice in rounds until the flowerettes come loose.

The broccoli can also be sliced lengthwise as pictured. The interior of the
main stalk cut in strips and served raw
makes a rarely-met-with salad delicacy.

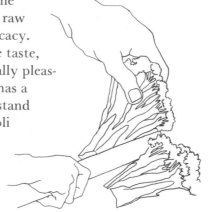

Broccoli will have a more subtle taste,
a bright green color and an especially pleasing texture if not overcooked. It has a
strong flavor of its own, so it can stand
being well seasoned. If the broccoli
flowerettes have bloomed yellow,
the broccoli is past its peak, and
is best served with a hearty
sauce or put into soup.

Boiled Broccoli

broccoli   boiling, salted water

Prepare the broccoli as above, then boil. Be sure to turn the heat
down after the water returns to boiling. The broccoli will be done
in six to eight minutes. Remove from the water when it's still bright
green and slightly crunchy. Serve with: butter, salt and pepper,
grated cheese or a sauce.

Steamed Broccoli

broccoli

Steam it. Serve plain, with grated cheese or a sauce.

Greek Steamed Broccoli

chunked broccoli   sliced onion   lots of garlic
black olives   olive oil

Sauté the garlic and onion in olive oil. Add the black olives and
broccoli, cover and steam until done, about eight minutes. Add a
little liquid if necessary. Season with salt and pepper. May also
be dressed with lemon butter and grated Parmesan.

Stir-Fried Broccoli

Broccoli stir-fries well by itself, or how about this—

onion   carrot   broccoli

Stir-fry onion, then add the carrot and broccoli and continue frying for 5-6 minutes. Add a little liquid if there is none, put on a lid and let it steam until done. A couple of minutes or so.

Chinese Broccoli

A stir-fry with added sauce.

for a pound and a half of broccoli:
3 T soy sauce   3 T hot water   2 t (freshly grated) ginger
2 t brown sugar or other sweetening

Stir-fry the broccoli for five minutes. Add the pre-mixed sauce. Put on a lid and let it boil-steam three to five minutes, until just tender.

Cauliflower

Cauliflower is a member of the cabbage family. Attached to the cauliflower core by short stalks is a sunburst array of white flowerettes. This white head is encased in green leaves, which almost universally are severed from the cauliflower before it is sold, but save them if you can. Best cooked, these greens make pretty fair eating, served with the cauliflower or separately. Wash the greens and cut once lengthwise first, then crosswise in segments, slicing more thinly closer to the core where the center rib is broader.

79

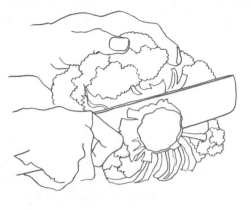

The tender white of the cauliflower makes fine eating cooked or raw, unless it's old and getting black spots, in which case it's better cooked.

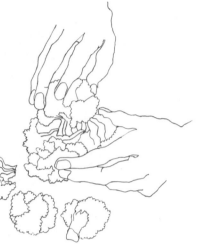

The sliced flowerettes are distinctive and attractive in salads and lightly cooked cauliflower is also an excellent salad ingredient.

When served hot, the cauliflower is most palatable when still slightly crunchy. Longer cooking will make the texture mushy and bring out an odorous, cabbagy taste.

Cauliflower Salad

A delightful switch from all those greens. If the cauliflower is to be cooked, start well ahead of time to give it a chance to cool.

cauliflower
take your pick: grated carrot, chopped parsley,
water cress, green onion, celery, pitted olives,
sliced tomato or pimento, chopped pickles
a dressing: oil-vinegar or sour cream

Cut raw cauliflower into small pieces. When using cooked cauliflower, boil or sauté-steam for just three to four minutes, so that the cauliflower still has plenty of body and chew left in it. Remove to bowl or tray which can be put in the refrigerator. Meanwhile cut up the other ingredients you will be using. Prepare a dressing and mix it with the salad ingredients. Leave in the refrigerator until serving time. The grated carrot and celery could go in with the cauliflower for the last half minute or minute of cooking.

Cauliflower Stir-Fry & Steam

I like this better than straight steaming. Frying it first brings out the nutty quality.

cauliflower   oil   salt

Prepare the cauliflower as shown in the illustrations. Make the pieces roughly the same size so that they will cook uniformly. Medium to small pieces will probably work best in this method of cooking. Stir-fry for about three to four minutes and then, adding liquid, steam for another four to five minutes until just tender. Check the seasoning and serve.

Stir-Fried Cauliflower with Celery & Walnuts

Bits of green and brown dot the whiteness of the cauliflower.

cauliflower   a stalk or two of celery
chopped walnuts   oil   salt

Prepare the same as the basic cauliflower stir-fry, giving the celery a brief sautéing before adding the cauliflower. Add the nuts toward the end of the steaming, or simply sprinkle them on top when serving.

The stir-frying can also be done with:
    —grated cheese in place of the walnuts
    —carrot in place of celery or in addition to celery
    —some soy sauce in the steaming liquid.

Boiled Cauliflower

It can be mushy or crisp and crunchy. Pay attention and get it right . . . the way you want it.

   cauliflower   boiling, salted water   possibly butter, pepper

For this recipe, the cauliflower can be cut in big pieces, but again try to get them of basically uniform size. Boil, and try a piece after about five minutes. Butter the cauliflower and season to taste.

Orange & Green on White

Grated cheddar melts right into the cauliflower.

   cauliflower   cheddar cheese   green onion or parsley

Boil cauliflower as in the preceeding recipe. After draining, remove it to a serving bowl, season and sprinkle generously with grated cheese and chopped green onion or parsley.

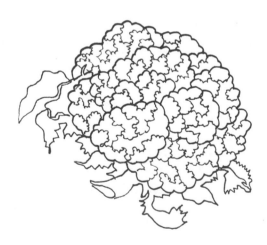

Warm Weather

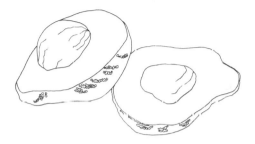

Avocado

Avocados are so incredibly rich in oils that they are almost the consistency of butter. This quality sometimes puts people off—the avocado gets left on the side of the plate. As avocados ripen, their skin turns from deep green to chocolate brown.

Cut the avocado lengthwise all the way around and then twist open and remove the pit. If serving whole, sliced or in chunks, peel the skin off. If mashing, scoop the pulp out with a spoon. Mashed avocado tends to turn brown very quickly from oxidation; lemon juice can retard or prevent this process.

Avocado on the Half-Shell

Half an unpeeled avocado per person. Arrange the halved avocados on a platter with lemon wedges. Serve with salt or soy sauce handy. Eat with a spoon.

Avocado chunks are good in salads, cooked greens, omelettes. If you like avocado you'll find lots of uses. For instance:

Avocado Deviled Eggs

> *hard boiled eggs*   *avocado*   *salt, pepper*   *seasonings*

Cut the eggs in half lengthwise and remove the yolks. Mash the yolks with the avocado. Season with salt and pepper, a bit of garlic or dry mustard. Mound the mixture back into the whites.

Guacamole

a traditional Mexican appetizer

avocado   lemon juice   salt, pepper   garlic

Other possible ingredients are: minced onion, minced green peppers, chopped tomato, sour cream.

Mash and season avocado with salt and pepper. Season to taste with lemon juice and garlic. Add optionals if available and desired. Best served with crispy fried corn tortilla wedges (*fritos*).

Avocado sauce is good with greens, broccoli, cauliflower and other vegetables. Season the mashed avocado with lemon juice, salt and pepper, then beat in an egg. Add to the vegetables for the last minute of cooking.

Avocado, sliced or spread, is excellent on sourdough French bread, plain or with lemon juice and salt and pepper. It can be the spread for a cheese, lettuce and tomato sandwich.

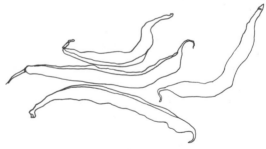

Green Beans,
String Beans & Wax Beans

Green beans are very fine if they are on the young and tender side. Younger beans have a smooth green skin and are about the diameter of a pencil. They can be easily steamed or sautéed. Older beans have a more wrinkled skin, get as big as a finger and will have many more strings attached. If time is not taken to cut them, they're probably best boiled or stewed. So many of the green beans in the markets are monstrous and tough, and must be cooked for ages to be chewable. More weight per bean patch, right?

The bean has a stem at one end and comes to a point at the other. On a young bean only the stem need be removed. You can always try a bean or two to see if the pointed (blossom) end is tender. The best and most thorough way to remove the tips is by hand. Snap off just the tip, or if the end of the bean feels pretty well dried out, snap off a larger section. Snap the tip off to the side, and if it's attached to some string, draw the end down the side of the bean, removing the string. If part of a bean is moldy, the other sections are nonetheless still good and they'll be sad if you don't make use of them. Cutting green beans in half lengthwise or in long, thin strips adds to their tenderness and flavor. This cut is fairly difficult and time-consuming, so undertake it only when you have time and energy to spare.

Sautéed Green Beans

green beans   oil or butter   salt

Use either tender whole beans or cut up larger beans. Follow the usual method for sautéing. Stir-fry the green beans for four to five minutes, then cover and steam until the beans are bright green and just tender. If using butter for frying, it's best to have some oil with it and not get the pan too hot. Check the seasoning and serve.

Almond Green Beans

Add almonds to the above recipe. Most people prefer the almonds toasted and slivered. Mix in half of the nuts with the green beans and sprinkle the other half on top.

Tomato Green Beans

Bean green and tomato red are wonderfully complimentary, with or without the cheese.

(a bit of onion)   green beans   tomato   grated cheese

Slice or dice the onion. String the beans and cut them lengthwise, or in lengthy diagonal cross-sections. Section the tomato. Grate the cheese. Cheddar, Jack and Parmesan are all good in this dish. Stir-fry the onion for a minute. Add the green beans and continue stir-frying for another three or four minutes. Place the tomato wedges on top of the beans, cover, turn the heat down and let steam for about five minutes or until the beans are tender to your bite. Check the seasoning, mix in some of the grated cheese and sprinkle the rest on top.

variations: garlic   herbs

If you're fond of garlic add it to the frying onions or green beans. Sprinkle crushed thyme, basil, marjoram, dill or what have you on top of the tomatoes.

Boiled Green Beans

This way takes care of the tougher green beans. Get them out soon enough and they'll still be bright green.

green beans   boiling salted water

Prepare the green beans. Put them in the boiling water and cook for six to eight minutes. Look sharp, unless you prefer your beans dull and mushy. Have a sample bite and take the beans off when they're still *slightly* chewy. These beans can be seasoned with butter, salt, pepper, herbs, and—

Cheese on Beans

cheddar cheese   boiled green beans

Grate the cheese or cut it in matchstick pieces. Mix it with the drained green beans, season to taste and serve. This dish can sit in the oven awhile, especially if the green beans were drained while they still had a bit of crunch left in them.

Marinated Green Bean Salad

boiled green beans   oil and vinegar dressing

Marinate the beans in the seasoned dressing for an hour or more.

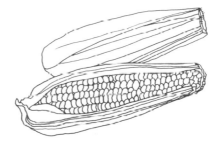

Sweet Corn

Corn is really a grain, though it is often served as a vegetable. Some folks are such connoisseurs that they have been known to have the water boiling as the corn is picked. They run it into the house, shucking it along the way. Plop, plop, splash, splash! They just love that fresh corn—cooked only three to five minutes, so it's still a little nutty, doused with butter and sprinkled with salt and pepper. They'll be chomping away at it less than ten minutes after they separated the poor babe from its mother stalk, every so often pausing to ask you, "Ain neva had corn that good, eh boy?" You have to own up and confess, "Man, corn was never like this." Most of us don't live next door to a corn field, so we'd have a long run to get the corn home. May as well enjoy what we can get. Nearby.

Corn on the Cob

corn   boiling, salted water   butter, salt

Shuck the corn by removing the leafy wrapping and the thready corn silks. The stem where there's no kernels may be broken off or left on for a handle. The ear may also be broken in half, if you prefer. Drop in the boiling, salted water and cook three to five minutes. Pick out with tongs or drain through a colander or strainer. Serve with butter, salt and pepper. Or soy sauce. The boiling, salted water can be half milk, using regular milk or adding powdered. Milk-fed corn.

Corn on the cob may also be baked in the oven. Leave the shucks on to retain moisture, and bake for 15-20 minutes at about 350-400°. It's ready when the outer leaves are beginning to turn brown. Peel back the shucks to use for a handle (country style) or just pull them off. Pull the silks off the end of the ear in a bunch.   Serve as desired. This method retains flavor and nutrients lost in boiling.

Whether the corn is cooked or raw, the kernels can be removed. Stand the corn upright in a wide bowl, and holding the upper end, cut downwards along the cob. Rotate the cob and repeat.

Corn Salad

cooked corn   mayonnaise   vinegar   salt, pepper
choice of: peppers, tomato, cold cooked beets

Cut the kernels off the cob. Cut other vegetables into salad pieces. Dress with the mayonnaise seasoned to taste with vinegar, salt and pepper. Using an oil-vinegar dressing will show off the colors better.

Mixed Vegetables with Corn

cooked corn
choice of: onion, peppers, zucchini, tomato, green beans

Cut the kernels off the cob. Slice the other vegetables for sautéing. Stir-fry the onion and green beans, if using them, for several minutes. Add the remaining ingredients and steam for about five minutes. Season with Tabasco sauce or a bit of basil or oregano.

Corn Kernals in Soup

Raw or cooked corn-on-the-cob can be used. Cut the kernels off the cob and add to soup. For instance, add water, stock or milk to the Mixed Vegetables with Corn, above.

Cucumber

Cucumber is the smallest, plainest, least sweet melon. There are many varieties, all with a fleshy interior covered with a waxy, usually tough exterior. If the skin is bitter, peel the cucumber before serving. Otherwise the peeling is optional, or you can peel it in length-wise strips leaving decorative ribs of green peel on the cucumber. Like any melon, a cucumber is mostly water and is quite refreshing in hot weather. Cucumbers are, of course, frequently pickled: sweet, sour, dill, bread'n'butter. Fresh cucumber is almost always served raw—in salads, side dishes and cold soups. Did you know they can also be cooked?

Cucumbers are usually cut into rounds, but they may be even better cut in lengthwise strips or chunks.

Dressed Cucumber

cucumber   lime juice   tabasco sauce

Cut the cucumber and dress it with lime juice and a sprinkling of Tabasco sauce.

—Marinate or dress with 1 T sugar, 2 t vinegar, 1½ T soy sauce.
—Marinate or dress with oil-vinegar dressing.

Cucumbers have a great deal of water, so the flavor of the cucumbers and of the dressing will be somewhat more concentrated if the cucumbers are salted. (See p. 12 if you have some question about this procedure.) Sprinkle salt on the cucumbers, weight them and let stand for half an hour or longer. Pour off the accumulated liquid and save it for soup. Taste the cucumbers and if they are too salty, rinse them off before adding the dressing.

Cucumber & Canteloupe Salad

This salad could be done with just the cucumbers.

cucumber   canteloupe   parsley or watercress   salt, mint

Slice or chunk the cucumber and salt it as described above. Mix the drained cucumbers with pieces of canteloupe, add generous amounts of parsley or watercress (if you like them), and season with salt and mint.

—In place of canteloupe: grapes, sliced peaches, plums, apricots, other melons, tomatoes.
—Sliced green onion or minced yellow onion can also be used to season this salad, especially if the fruit is being omitted.
—Dressing for cucumber salad can be based on sour cream or yogurt, made tart with vinegar, orange, lemon or lime. Salt some and pepper with: hot sauce, garlic, dry mustard, cumin or pepper. Or season with: tarragon, basil or dill.

Cooked Cucumbers

cucumbers   sour cream or cream cheese   salt, pepper
salted water or stock   parsley

If the peels aren't too tough or bitter they can be left on. Otherwise peel the cucumbers, then cut them in half crosswise and quarters lengthwise. Simmer in the salted water until verging on tenderness, about four or five minutes? Drain them and dress with sour cream or with slightly thinned cream cheese. Season. Caraway and chervil are herb possibilities along with dill, basil and tarragon. Heat briefly in oven or double boiler if necessary.

Steamed Cucumbers

cucumbers   salt

Peel the cucumbers if the skin is tough or bitter and remove the seeds if they are tough. Section the cucumber into two or three inch lengths and then cut into strips. Place in a durable bowl and cover the bowl closely with a plate. Weight the plate with a stone or possibly a couple more plates. Place the covered bowl in a larger pot with an inch of water in it. Cover this pot. Heat to boiling and steam for twenty-five minutes. This could also be done in a double boiler with a tight-fitting or weighted lid.

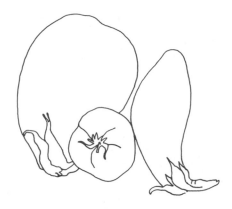

Eggplant

Eggplant has a pulpy white interior covered with a shiny purple skin, which is edible. To prepare, pull or cut off the stem and cut the eggplant in rounds or half-rounds, section like a potato and cut in chunks, or cut in strips.

Eggplant takes some tending to. Bitter and acidy, it is frequently salted and allowed to stand for an hour or more after being cut up so that some liquid is drawn out, giving the eggplant a milder taste. (See salting instructions, p. 12.) After salting, dry the pieces with a paper towel or a clean dish towel. The pieces of eggplant will brown better when sautéed if well-dried first.

One of the meatiest of vegetables, eggplant is a cook's delight. It is one vegetable that can stand lengthy cooking and it sponges up other flavors while keeping its own. It loves oil, garlic, tomato, Parmesan cheese, as well as soy sauce, ginger and curry. Sumptuous.

Sautéed Eggplant

eggplant rounds or chunks   oil   salt

Stir-fry the eggplant for five minutes or so, possibly a little less if a lengthy baking is also intended. Add a small amount of water, cover and steam another five minutes. Sprinkle with parsley and oregano.

Variations on the basic recipe:

—Sauté some onion and garlic for a minute before adding the eggplant.

—Sauté the eggplant for five minutes and remove from the pan. Sauté slices of green pepper and celery for two minutes, then return the eggplant, cover and steam over moderate heat for four to five minutes.

—Add mushrooms or chopped olives.

—Add tomatoes or a tomato sauce to any of the above for the steaming part.

—Sprinkle with grated cheese: Parmesan, mozzarella, cheddar, Swiss or cream cheese.

Peas

I can remember the first time I had fresh peas. How wonderful! Opening the pods, running a thumb down the inside—out jumped the peas and the fresh green smells of sun and earth. I can't even remember how they tasted, only the joy of discovery, each pod a treasure house of peas, and how many would there be?

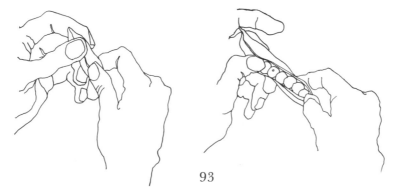

Peas, rather like beans, need water. They're fairly dry and starchy to start with, but given a few minutes of cooking, they become moist, brilliant green; delicious by themselves, floating in soups, dotting stews or combination vegetable dishes.

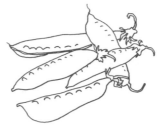

Snow Peas

These peas are flat and the pod is edible. They are used extensively in Oriental cooking for their shape, color and flavor. Snap off the stem before using. Raw, they are suitable for salads, and they can be easily sautéed, steamed or briefly boiled. Don't over-cook. Add to soups just five minutes before serving.

Fresh, Green & Succulent Peas

Some people knock boiling vegetables, but with care and mindfulness, the peas can be done to juicy tenderness and you will have some stock for the next pot of soup.

> *peas   boiling, salted water   (butter)   salt, pepper*

Shell the peas, and when the salted water is boiling, drop them in. Leave the heat on high, put on a lid and stay nearby. The peas will be done in just three to five minutes. When the water comes back to a boil, turn the heat down and try a couple of peas. Have a colander or strainer set in a pot for draining, and when the peas are just on the verge of tenderness, drain them. To serve, toss with melted butter, salt and pepper to taste.

Frosted Peas with Green Onion

Funny, peas were the only vegetable I'd eat for a long time, but my father-in-law never liked peas until he ate these.

peas   boiling, salted water   sour cream
green onion   salt, pepper

Shell the peas and cook them as in the preceding recipe. Slice the green onions thinly and mix with the sour cream. When the peas have been drained, mix them with the sour cream and green onions, season to taste with the salt and pepper. This dish may be kept warm in a double boiler for five or ten minutes. A bit of thyme or basil goes well here. It's not the same, but yogurt could be used in place of the sour cream.

Peas Roll in Carrots & Mushrooms

peas   carrots   mushrooms   oil, salt, water

Shell the peas. Wash the carrots and cut in ovals, half rounds or matchsticks. Rinse and slice the mushrooms. Sauté the carrots for a couple of minutes. Add the mushrooms and peas, sprinkle on salt, pour in a quarter cup of water or stock, cover, turn the heat down to medium low. Check in about four minutes. Are they tender? Is there enough water left? Stir and continue steaming a few minutes until the peas are just tender. Stop cooking before their color begins to dull.

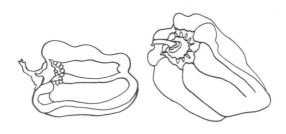

Green Pepper, Bell Pepper

The shell or pod of the green pepper, which encloses the seeds, is the edible part. Actually, green peppers are not-yet-ripe red peppers, or possibly yellow peppers. Most peppers are picked while still green, but the red ones occasionally show up in markets and roadside stands. They are sweeter and more mellow than the green ones. Peppers are added to salads both for their bite and their deep green or bright red color. They are frequently cooked with tomatoes and other summer vegetables.

Prepare the pepper by first cutting in half lengthwise and removing the stem, seeds and pith from each half. Then knock the open halves on the cutting board so that any stray seeds are dislodged. Remove the seeds from all the peppers you will be using and clean the cutting surface before beginning to slice or chop the peppers.

The pepper halves may be cut in a variety of ways, including lengthwise strips, diagonal strips, diagonal slivers, wedges. If the halves are again halved, the slivers may be cut more easily. For diced green pepper, cut the strips or slivers crosswise into smaller pieces.

Green Pepper in Salads

Bell peppers are good in the following salads: lettuce, tomato, cauliflower, carrot, cottage cheese, bean or potato. In salads, peppers are best if they are cut into thin strips. This way they are easy to chew and no one gets too big a dose in one bite.

Cooked Green Peppers with Vegetables or Grains

Peppers are often used alone or along with onions, for "enlivening" or brightening vegetable and grain dishes. They may be used in soups, casseroles, omelettes or combinations. Cut the peppers in squares, wide strips or wedges, and sauté for a minute before adding.

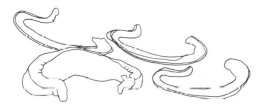

Tomatoes & Green Peppers

If they're red peppers how about some yellow tomatoes?

    green peppers   tomatoes   onions   salt, oil, seasoning

Cut the peppers into wide strips, wedges or squares, section the tomatoes into eighths, and slice or section the onions. Sauté the onions for a minute or two, add the peppers and stir-fry for another minute. Then add the tomatoes and seasoning, turning the heat down. Cover and cook for just a few minutes, until the tomatoes are thoroughly heated. Peppers will stay bright green when given only brief cooking.

    If you're using olive oil, season with sweet basil, sage or thyme. When using corn, peanut or sesame oil, try a little fresh ginger and soy sauce. Garlic can be used in either case.

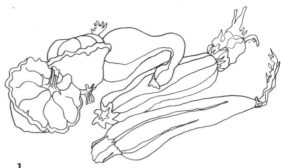

Summer Squashes

Zucchini, Crookneck and Scalloped

Beauteous squashes: straight and deep green, yellow with thin neck spreading to plumpness, pale green, round and scalloped; they are full of delicate, earthy flavor unless cooked into mushiness. Quickly stir-fried or steamed, these squashes can stand alone, be lightly seasoned with herbs, or be combined with eggplant, tomato, greens, onions, carrots, cheese. Raw and thinly sliced, they can make a fine addition to salads, Give them a light scrubbing, trim off the ends and cut according to intended use. The rolling cut is especially good for cooking. Mild flavor—season lightly.

Zucchini and Crookneck squash can be cut in any of the ways shown for cutting carrots. Scalloped squash (officially Cymling, sometimes "Summer") can be cut in half and sliced like an onion, sectioned like a tomato, or chunked like a potato.

Raw Summer Squashes

These vegetables have a fine, soft crunch when eaten raw. The larger ones with tougher seeds are usually better cooked. Cut into strips, chunks or ovals, and arrange decoratively on a plate. Sprinkle with salt or serve with salt for dipping. For more tang, toss with lemon juice and lemon peel, or with a lemon dressing.

Boiled or Steamed Squashes

Summer squashes are quite good this way if you can get them off the fire before they're mush—just five or six minutes, depending on the size. Larger chunks can be cooked slightly longer. Toss with butter, salt and pepper, or dress with a mild sauce.

Baked Summer Squash

Bake them whole, cut in half, or cut into strips. Brush with oil. Bake twenty to thirty minutes, depending on size. Sprinkle with grated Parmesan cheese. Layer with tomatoes and cheese?

Stir-Fried Summer Squash

Squash doesn't have to be all squashed. Lightly cooked, it has a slight crunch and a delicate earthy flavor.

zucchini, crookneck, scalloped squash   oil   salt

Wash the squash and cut with the rolling cut if possible. Otherwise cut in rounds or ovals. Then stir-fry for three to four minutes, put a lid on, and turn the heat down for a minute or two. There will usually be enough water from the squash so that none need be added. Check the seasoning and serve.

Spiced Zucchini

Add salt, turmeric sparingly, and finely chopped onion to heated oil, stir for a minute, add the zucchini, stir, cover and cook for five to seven minutes. Garnish with chopped nuts.

Squash with Onion & Celery

onion   celery   squash

Slice both the onion and celery fairly thinly. Cook as in the preceding recipe, starting with the onion, then adding the celery. Cook briefly and add the squash.

Squash with Green Pepper & Tomato

Same as above. Fry the pepper pieces first, then add zucchini, and after stir-frying three or four minutes, put on the tomatoes, cover, turn the heat down a bit and cook until the zucchini is tender to taste and the tomato steaming hot.

Stir-Fried Squash Otherwise
  —Try it with olive oil.
  —Add a little lemon juice for flavoring.
  —Season mildly with herbs: basil, tarragon, marjoram, oregano, chopped parsley. Just one'll do.
  —Season lightly with soy sauce.
  —How about some grated cheese? Like onion, green pepper, squash, tomato, with Parmesan. Or just zucchini with cheddar?

Tomatoes

Tomatoes are one of the most versatile, most commercially-utilized vegetables, appearing in salads, soups, sauces, paste and catsup. Their hearty red color and tangy flavor, enlivening and spicing, top off many a dish. The best tomato is ripe, unwashed, right off an unsprayed vine: plump, warm with summer sun, fleshy, it parts about the teeth, tender on the gums, juices rushing out flooding the mouth with uncommon succulence. Anything else is a lesser imitation, pale in comparison, but good for what it is. Tomatoes can stand alone or blend with almost any vegetable.

Generally I like to cook fresh tomatoes as little as possible; I use canned tomato products for making sauces. Rinse off the tomatoes, trim out the little core and then cut in segments or slice in rounds. A tomato is quite acidy, so use a sharp stainless steel knife if possible; a bread knife often works well.

When using canned tomato products, keep in mind that tomato paste is much stronger than tomato sauce or canned tomatoes. Tomato

100

paste is usually used diluted with water, while canned tomatoes and tomato sauce are used undiluted. Tomato paste can be added to soups to deepen their color and to lend acidity, or tartness, to their flavor.

Tomato Salad

The simplest tomato salad: tomatoes cut up in a bowl. For a more elaborate tomato salad, try this.

    tomatoes   salt   olive oil   oregano, basil, or tarragon

Slice or section the tomatoes. Arrange slices on a platter and sprinkle on olive oil, salt and herb. Put sections in bowl and toss with remaining ingredients.

Marinated Tomato Salad

    tomatoes   dressing

For this you make a full-blown oil-vinegar dressing with herbs and marinate the tomatoes in it before serving them.

Baked Tomatoes

    tomatoes   olive oil   garlic   grated cheese

Cut off top, sprinkle with loads of minced garlic. Drizzle on some olive oil, about a tablespoon per tomato. Bake thirty minutes at 350°, removing from oven to baste once or twice. Sprinkle on Parmesan or grated cheddar for the last five minutes. These can also be sprinkled with tarragon, parsley and coriander.

Some Other Vegetables

These are vegetables which I have handled very little, or those which are fairly uncommon in this country. An increasingly wide variety of vegetables is now available in supermarkets. Even though you don't know of a particular dish using these vegetables, it is still possible to bring some home and try them out: sautéed, steamed, boiled or baked. Give them a taste. Experiment.

What follows are brief discussions of several vegetables, both common and uncommon, which have not yet been dealt with. Only those vegetables with which I have had personal experience are included.

Burdock Root

Gobo in Japanese. This is a long slender root vegetable with a fine earthy flavor. Gobo should be scrubbed, but needn't be peeled. It is most often cut in slender strips, using the Chinese rolling cut. Being somewhat tough, it needs about twice as much cooking as carrots do. Sometimes it is boiled for ten minutes before being added to mixed vegetable dishes. Here's a recipe which is one of our favorites:

Kimpira

>   one burdock root per person   ½ large carrot per person
>   toasted sesame seeds   corn and sesame oil   soy sauce

Wash the vegetables, then cut in long, thin pieces using the chinese rolling cut. Toast the sesame seeds. The burdock and carrot are to be semi-deep fried, so put an eighth-inch or so of oil into a frying pan and heat until almost smoking. Cook the burdock for four to five minutes, then add the carrot and continue cooking for another four to five minutes, until the vegetables begin to get tender. Remove from the oil and drain on paper towels. Heat a wok or frying pan and stir-fry the vegetables, adding the soy sauce and sesame seeds. The vegetables will be crisp, with a soy sauce glaze.

Celery Root

Also known as celeriac, this root comes from a slightly different variety of celery than the one raised for its stalks. Because of its surface irregularities it is fairly difficult to wash, and it can be peeled or not, as you prefer. Slice it for sautéing or chunk it for steaming or boiling. Cook it like carrots or turnips. Cooked and cut into matchstick pieces, it is often used as a salad ingredient.

Jerusalem Artichokes

These can be cooked as potatoes are: sautéed, boiled, baked, deep-fried. They can be mixed with other vegetables and can be eaten raw in salads. They can also be substituted for water chestnuts in Oriental cooking.

Jicama

This is a large root vegetable which is imported from Mexico. It can be finely cut for salads, sautéed or boiled.

Parsnips

These are a white root vegetable which, when raw, smell a great deal like carrots. Not so good raw, they can be cooked like carrots or turnips. Here's a recipe which uses both turnips and parsnips:

Parsnips, Turnips, Mushrooms

parsnips   turnips   mushrooms
oil   salt   lemon   water

Cut parsnips with rolling cut or in ovals. Cut turnips in quarters lengthwise, then in thick slices crosswise. Slice the mushrooms. Put ¼ cup
water and juice of ½ a lemon in one pot on a low flame, ready to
receive the vegetables as they are sautéed. Then sauté the turnips
for three minutes and remove to waiting pot. Next, sauté the parsnips for three minutes and add them to the turnips. Put a lid on
this pot so they can steam. Brown the mushrooms, add to the other
vegetables, and stir them up. Are the turnips and parsnips tender
yet? Maybe another few minutes.

Chinese Greens

These include *bok choy, wong bok, shingiku,* mustard cabbage, and
so forth. Refer to the section on greens for some recipe suggestions.

Brussels Sprouts

These aren't sprouts in the same sense as bean sprouts or alfalfa
sprouts, but are more like very small heads of cabbage. To prepare
them for cooking, remove any outer leaves which are yellow or
wilted. The bottom of the core can also be trimmed off. The
Brussels sprouts can be boiled whole or cut in halves or quarters
lengthwise to be sauté-steamed. In either case may I suggest that
they not be overcooked. Here's one recipe:

Brussels Sprouts with Cheese

Brussels sprouts   orange juice   oil or butter
salt, pepper   grated cheese

Cut the Brussels sprouts in halves or quarters lengthwise and sauté them in oil or butter for three to four minutes. Add enough orange juice to cover the bottom of the pan and then add a few tablespoons more. Stir the Brussels sprouts, cover and simmer for another two or three minutes. Season with some salt and pepper. Are they tender yet? Sprinkle with grated cheese before serving.

Green Tomatoes

Since these can be strongly acidic, they are sometimes cut and salted like eggplant. Then a thorough cooking. Delicious fried or broiled, they are also often used in relishes.

Sea Vegetables

These are more widely used in the Orient than in the West, but they are increasingly available in large supermarkets among the imported foods. They are a fine source of trace minerals and a flavorful addition to any diet. The most common varieties are dulse, *hijiki* (or *hiziki*), *wakame, kombu,* and *nori.*

Nori

Nori comes in thin sheets. The only preparation required is toasting. Wave the sheets of nori, one at a time, about 5-6 inches above a medium hot burner until they start to wrinkle. The toasted sheets can then be crumbled for use as a garnish on grains or soups. They are also used to wrap rice balls *(sushi).*

Wakame & Dulse

Rinse these once before soaking, then soak for fifteen to thirty minutes until they swell up. Strain and save the soaking liquid—since it is full of ocean flavor and nutrition. *Wakame* has a tough string attached along its length. Even when raw, this string should be soft enough to chew after soaking. If not, pull it off by hand. Lay out strips of soaked wakame or dulse and section into one inch pieces before using.

Hijiki

Hijiki tends to be especially gritty, so when rinsing it, pick it off the top of the rinsing water carefully so that the grit stays at the bottom of the bowl. Soak the same as wakame or dulse and then repeat the rinsing process. Hijiki comes in small, slender pieces and need not be sectioned before using.

Kombu

This comes in thick sheets, which make an excellent soup stock. No rinsing or soaking is necessary. A three by three inch piece of *kombu* will flavor about a quart of stock. After cooking for stock it can be cut in strips for addition to the soup.

All of the above sea vegetables are excellent used in vegetable, bean and grain dishes, as well as added to soups. Cooked hijiki is also quite good in salads.

Sea Vegetables with Earth Vegetables

Seaweed cooked by itself makes a potent dish. For a milder dish try this:

> *seaweed, any of the preceding, prepared as described*
> *(about 2 ounces for 4 people)*
> *onion   carrot   seaweed soaking water*
> *soy sauce   salt   (ginger)   (garlic)*

Wash the seaweed and start it soaking while dicing the onion and carrot. Finish preparing the seaweed for cooking. Sauté the onion for a minute, then continue sautéing with the carrot for a couple of minutes. Add the seaweed and sauté for ten minutes. Add a cup of the soaking water, cover, and simmer for fifteen to twenty minutes. Season with soy sauce, salt, and some freshly grated ginger if it's available. Keep the seasoning mild if you want to enjoy the ocean flavor. Cook a few more minutes.

Other Basic Ingredients

Fruits & Dried Fruits

Fruits are the final results of a plant's labor, accumulations of
energy, food for seeds. Some people are fond of fruits and miss
them dearly when they're not available, while others seem content
without them. They are a deceptively potent food: refreshing,
invigorating, cleansing. Best fresh, cool and raw in hot weather,
hot, thick and sweet in cold weather; fruits can start a day, pick
up an afternoon, complete a dinner.

Citrus Fruits

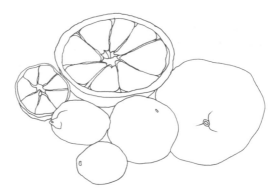

Oranges, Lemons, Limes, Grapefruit and Tangerines

These fruits are noted for their tangy juices and a refreshing balance of sweet and sour. Their juices can be used in place of vinegar in salad dressings and in vegetable dishes, such as winter squashes.

They also will preserve the color and freshness of newly sliced apples, carrots, peaches, bananas, avocados and other fruits and vegetables. Soups which are overly sweet or bland can be perked up with lemon or lime juice, or with some grated orange or lemon peel, which is also useful in salad dressings, sauces and pickles.

Both oranges and grapefruit can be peeled with the fingers, or with a sharp, stainless steel knife. Peel around the fruit, just below the surface of the peel. It's best to use a stainless steel knife when cutting or peeling any fruit, because carbon steel will react with a fruit's natural acidity, turning the cut fruit black in spots. A bread knife works well for slicing citrus rounds.

How to Mince Lemon or Orange Peel:
One way is to grate the orange or lemon on the finest grate of a four-way grater. Here's another way: With a vegetable peeler take off the peel in strips from one end of the fruit to the other. Cut the strips lengthwise, and then cut them crosswise as finely

as possible. Mince them some more if the peel is not yet fine enough.

Orange, or Grapefruit, Sprout Salad

oranges (grapefruit or tangerines)   alfalfa sprouts

First peel the fruit, then slice or chunk it. Mix it with the alfalfa sprouts, adding a few raisins if it's not sweet enough.

This could also be done with Thin-Slice Cabbage Salad instead of sprouts.

Grapefruit Avocado Salad

grapefruit   avocado

Peel and section the grapefruit. Peel and cut the avocado in lengthwise strips. Dress with an oil and vinegar or oil and citrus dressing. Oranges or tangerines could also be used in place of, or in addition to, the grapefruit.

Orange-slice Dessert

half an orange or more per person   dates   coconut

Peel the oranges and slice in rounds. Pit the dates and slice them crosswise. Arrange the orange slices in dessert dishes and sprinkle with the dates and coconut.

—Raisins or sliced figs can be used in place of the dates.

—Banana rounds or ovals could be used in place of dates or coconut.

Baked Grapefruit

I guess this sounds strange to some people, but I grew up with it.

grapefruit   sugar or honey

Cut the grapefruit in half and, if you want to, cut around each section to loosen it. Put a spoonful or so of sugar or honey in the middle of the grapefruit halves and bake them face up on cookie sheets for ten minutes at 350°.

Spring & Summer Fruits

Berries, Peaches, Apricots, Nectarine, Plums, Grapes, Cherries

Most summer fruits have skins which are eaten along with the fruit, though peaches, with their characteristic fuzz, are frequently peeled. To accomplish this, dip the peaches in boiling water for ten seconds, or longer if the peaches are somewhat under ripe. Let them cool slightly and then peel by hand, or use a knife to pull up the skin. Aside from grapes and berries and cherries, these fruits can all be sectioned by cutting from pole to pole, down to the pit. If necessary, loosen the section from the pit by twisting the knife.

These fruits are at their best simply washed and eaten. Berries dye the hands red or purple. Peach juice runs down the chin and forearm. Sweet stickiness abounds. On occasions calling for more civility:

Fruit Compote

berries   peaches   apricots   nectarines
plums   grapes   cherries

Wash and slice the fruits. If preferred, peel the peaches first. The apricots could be left in halves, the berries or grapes whole. Mix the fruits together and for extra juice and flavor add:
    —Citrus or other fruit juice.
    —Fruit wine, sweet vermouth, brandy, or rum.
    —If you'd like the fruit sweeter, add some sugar or honey.
    —Garnish with fresh mint leaves.

For *Yogurt Fruit Sundae*, add the washed and cut fruit to yogurt. Sweeten as you find desirable. Chill until time to serve.
    —One final variation would be to serve the fruit in champagne. Cheers!

Peaches & Cream

peaches   whipping cream   vanilla   cinnamon

Peel and slice the peaches. Beat the cream until it is fluffy rather than liquidy, but not so much that it turns to butter. Flavor it with a little vanilla, rum, or brandy. Arrange the slices in dessert dishes and spoon the whipped cream on top. It doesn't take much—a little goes a long way. Sprinkle cinnamon or freshly grated nutmeg on top of the cream.
    —Berries, apricots, nectarines, plums, and grapes can replace or complement the peaches.
    —Cream cheese can substitute for whipping cream. It's simple and wonderfully pleasing. If using cream cheese, leave it out of the refrigerator for a while. Work it with a spoon or fork to soften. Carefully mix in milk a spoonful at a time, until the cream cheese is the consistency of whipped cream. Flavor with vanilla, rum, or brandy. Use as above.
    —The whipped cream can also be topped with shaved chocolate, coconut, or chopped nuts.

Pale Green Snow

This grape salad could also be a dessert.

> *grapes, thompson seedless   sour cream   honey*
> *vanilla   nutmeg or cinnamon*
> *(grated lemon peel)   (walnuts)*

Remove the grapes from the stems and rinse them off. Sweeten the sour cream with honey and season lightly with vanilla. Add spice and possibly lemon peel. Set aside some of the grapes for a garnish and combine the remainder with the sour cream mixture, along with some chopped walnuts if you have them. Chill until time to serve, then garnish with the extra grapes.

—The sweetened sour cream is an excellent accompaniment to the other summer fruits as well, particularly berries.

—Yogurt can be substituted for sour cream.

Cooked Summer Fruit

Good for breakfast! This is also an appropriate way to prepare fruit which is no longer fresh looking, but not yet strongly sour or moldy.

> *any of the fruits in this section   sugar or honey*
> *water   cornstarch for thickening*

Wash, trim, and slice the fruit. Simmer it in an inch or two of water. Sweeten to taste with sugar, honey, or possibly dried fruit. Thicken with cornstarch dissolved in cold water. (One tablespoon cornstarch in one tablespoon cold water thickens one cup liquid. Start with a minimal amount, then add more if you want it thicker.) The fruit may not need to be thickened at all.

—Use cooked fruit in a fresh fruit compote?

(I'm leaving fruit pies to other standard works.)

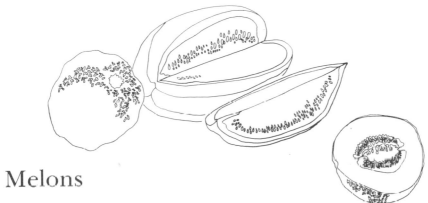

Melons

Cantaloupe, Honeydew, Casaba, Crenshaw, Watermelon

Sweet juiciness in frosty pulp. The high water content of melons
makes them the most refreshing of hot-weather fruits, but for the
same reason they are not suitable for cooking into sauces or pies.
Chill them in the refrigerator, in the creek, or in the shade. Cut out
a thick crescent and bite in. Don't you wish your mouth was bigger?

Melon Salad

melons   banana   grapes   mint   (coconut)

Cut open the melons and remove the seeds. Even with watermelon
this isn't too difficult—the seeds run in lines. Cut the skin away from
the pulp and then cut the pulp into chunks. Grapes or sliced bananas
may be added to melon salad, and the other spring-summer fruits
can go in too, but I like it better without citrus fruits. Season with
freshly chopped mint and top with coconut, if things are going that
way.

Canteloupe Fancies

Many people like to sprinkle salt on their melon. Here are some
other fancies.

cantaloupe   lemon juice   raw cashew butter

Cut the cantaloupe in halves or quarters and remove the seeds.
Drizzle on the lemon juice and mound on the cashew butter.

cantaloupe   yogurt and/or cottage cheese

Halve or quarter the cantaloupes and remove the seeds. Add the yogurt to the cottage cheese until it's creamy. Mound it up in the cantaloupe.

—Raisins, dates, or fig slices can be added to the yogurt-cottage cheese mixture.

—Fresh fruit pieces could garnish the cottage cheese-yogurt mixture.

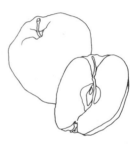

Apples, Pears & Bananas

These fruits are grouped together since they are, aside from citrus fruits, probably the most readily available fresh fruits during the fall and winter.

Pears and apples have crisper flesh than the summer fruits. The skins can be left on, but wash them well. To prepare them, cut in quarters lengthwise and cut out the stems and seeds. Slice the quarters lengthwise or diagonally.

Pears or Apples, Sliced

pears or apples   orange or lemon juice   bananas

Slice the pears or apples. Toss with orange or lemon juice. Mix in the banana slices.

Apple or Pear Salad

apples (pears)   grapefruit (oranges or tangerines)   mint

Slice the apple and section the grapefruit. Mix them together with some mint. Try Pippin apple with white grapefruit, or Red Delicious with pink grapefruit. Oranges or tangerines could also be used.

Hot Fruit

apples or pears   sugar, honey, dates, figs, or raisins   (lemon)

The fruit can be left in quarters for cooking. Put the cut-up fruit in a couple of inches of water. Add the sweetening—sugar, dates, figs, or raisins. Put on a lid and simmer-steam for fifteen to twenty minutes, until the fruit is soft, stirring a couple of times while it's cooking. If it's gotten too sweet, add some lemon juice or chopped lemon peel.

For *Apple (or Pear) Sauce,* slice the fruit before cooking. When it's soft, mash it.

—Stewed fruit or fruit sauce can be spiced. Cinnamon's probably the best. Add a bit of allspice, cloves, nutmeg or mace? The following is a variation of this recipe:

Prune-Apple Special

prunes   apples   raisins   cinnamon

After the prunes and raisins have stewed for thirty minutes, add sliced apple and heat for five minutes. Cook longer if you want the apples softer. Season with cinnamon.

Banana Split

One of our head cooks would frequently say, "Let them have Banana Splits for breakfast." Here's what he meant:

banana   yogurt   (cottage cheese)

Mix sliced bananas with yogurt. Stretch the yogurt with cottage cheese if necessary, or if you like it. Other fruits, most notably stewed dried apricots, can be added.

Fried Bananas

bananas   oil or butter

Cut the bananas in half crosswise, and then in half lengthwise. Fry in butter or in a generous amount of oil.

Simple Banana Dessert

bananas   orange juice   walnuts   coconut

Slice the bananas and mix them with the orange juice so that they won't darken. Arrange in dessert dishes with chopped walnuts and coconut.

Pineapple, Persimmon, Papaya, Guava

These can be added raw to any of the raw fruit dishes. Persimmon is sometimes rather chalky, so it may need to be cooked. Pineapple can also be cooked, while papaya and guava are ordinarily eaten uncooked.

Dried Fruits

A source of concentrated, chewy sweetness, dried fruits make excellent snacks (often mixed with nuts or seeds), good desserts, and combine well with fresh ingredients.

We've been sun-drying our own fruit at Tassajara for a few years now, since we're lucky enough to have the hot, dry summer weather necessary for this process. The main problem we've had has been raccoons—once an entire rack of drying bananas disappeared.

You'll find many sources of information on home-drying fruits f you look—remember, though, that home-dried fruit is seldom as plump and moist as the sulphur-treated kind prepared commercially.

Raisins, Dates & Figs

These are lumped together as the least expensive, most often used dried fruits. There are several kinds of dates, which vary somewhat in size, sweetness and texture—from almost creamy to fairly chewy. There are basically two kinds of figs available in this country: Black Mission and various types of "white" figs, most notably Calimyrna. Black Mission and dried domestic Calimyrna figs are usually fairly soft, while imported dried white figs, which often come strung on a twig, are comparatively tough. When sliced figs are called for, use the softer variety.

Dried Fruit Dessert: If I haven't anything else and the occasion calls for a dessert, I put out these dried fruits with some almonds, walnuts or cashews.

Dried Fruit Snack: Serve the dried fruit with roasted peanuts or sunflower seeds.

For use in other dishes, dried figs and dates can be sliced.

In Salads: Dried fruits in modest amounts can complement many kinds of salads: carrot, lettuce, alfalfa sprout, cabbage, cottage cheese or fruit.

In Frostings or Fillings: Dates or figs are especially suited to this use. Barely cover them with water and cook until soft. Then mash them into a paste. It's good just like that, or it could be spiced with vanilla extract, cinnamon, orange peel.

Prunes, Apricots, Pears, Apples, Pineapple, Bananas, Coconut

I had my first dried banana two years ago. Talk about a potent, concentrated food! One thing to remember when eating dried fruit is that it's easy to overdo it. Often people who wouldn't consider eating ten plums sit down and eat ten prunes, or they eat two, three or four stewed dried pears when they wouldn't eat more than one fresh pear. Dried fruit can have a pretty strong effect.

Stewed Dried Fruit

Prunes are the most frequently stewed dried fruit, but apricots, pears and apples can also be used. (Stewed dried fruit is a back-packer's delight.)

dried fruit   water to cover and then some

Put the dried fruit in a pot and cover with an inch or two of water. Heat to boiling, then simmer until done. Apricots are the quickest, taking about ten minutes, while pears, prunes and apples take twenty to thirty.

Variations:
   —Cut a lemon in quarters lengthwise, then cut crosswise in thin slices. Add these to the stewing prunes.
   —Dried fruits can be mixed and cooked together until all are soft.
   —Quartered fresh apples can go in with stewing prunes.
   —We have used stewed dried fruit for pie and cookie fillings also.

Here's another idea:

Apricot Condiment

Good with rice dishes and curries.

dried apricots   banana   parsley   mint

Stew the apricots. Mash with banana and add generous amounts of minced parsley and mint.

120

Beans

Beans. What suffering the word evokes. Beans. When you couldn't afford meat. Oh beans! When you went camping. Beans!

Beans are not meat, they're beans: garbanzo, kidney, navy, soldier, white, black, red and pinto. Soy—which rarely remains as a bean. Split pea soup—thick, green, creamy and soothing. Try it with caraway seeds, with bacon pieces. Refried beans—greasy, soft, fragrant and filling. Uncooked lentils, a rainbow of browns, turn with cooking into one, deep mellow brown, the taste of earthen sunshine.

Beans are the overlooked jewels of the vegetable world. They sell at dirt cheap prices and are one of the best protein buys around. Beans and greens, beans with grains or nuts, with eggs or cheese—all are good protein combinations.

Beans take some getting used to, some familiarity. It's easy to say "beans don't agree with me," without having given yourself a chance to agree with them.

Cooking Beans

A Basic Outline

Preparing the beans: One cup of beans makes four average servings, either in a bean dish or in a soup. Spread out the measured beans so that you can poke through them and pick out any extraneous materials, particularly any small pebbles. Garbanzos, azuki, red, and black beans seem to be especially pebble-prone. Besides being a jarring surprise, pebbles are a genuine hazard to the teeth. Unless the beans are unusually dirty, they'll need just one rinsing to remove storage dust. Cover the beans in a pot or pan with water, stir them around by hand and pour the water off. Now the beans are ready for soaking or cooking.

Soaking the beans: Beans absorb water rather reluctantly. Soaking them in water before cooking reduces the cooking time by thirty minutes if simmering, and by five minutes if pressure cooking. Also, it seems good to give the beans several hours to get used to the water before the heat is turned on. Have the water cover the beans by a couple of inches when soaking starts. The beans can be soaked overnight or during the day, six to eight hours or longer. In very hot weather keep the soaking beans in a cool place or they will tend to sour.

Cooking the beans: As a rule, *no salt* is added until the beans are soft, since salt tends to draw the moisture out of things.

Remember, beans take time, or pressure, to cook.

If presoaked, pressure cook:
- *split peas and lentils*   ten minutes at 15 lb. pressure
- *others,*   fifteen minutes at 15 lb. pressure
- *except for soybeans*   twenty minutes at 15 lb. pressure
- *and garbanzo beans*   twenty-five minutes at 15 lb. pressure

If not presoaked, add five minutes cooking time at 15 lb. pressure.

For cooking without pressure, if presoaked, bring to boiling, then simmer:

—split peas and lentils	one hour
—others,	one and one-half hours
—except for soybeans	two hours
—and garbanzo beans	two and one-half hours

If not presoaked, add thirty minutes to these cooking times.

"Others" includes black-eyed peas, cranberry beans, navy (white) beans, red kidney, red, pinto, lima, great northern, pink, black, azuki, and mung beans. Garbanzo beans are also known as chickpeas.

The Basic Recipe

beans   water   salt

Prepare the beans for soaking or cooking. Add three times as much water as beans for a bean dish, and five times as much water if making soup. Soak, then cook until tender. If the beans are simmered rather than pressure cooked, it may be necessary to add more hot water as the cooking progresses. When the beans are tender, salt to taste. If you are not using a pressure cooker to cook the beans, you may wish to cook up a double batch and save some for later use.

Accompanying Beans

Vegetables in the bean pot. Beans and bean water relish the company of onions, celery and carrot. Here's how the vegetables can be added:

Pressure cook some diced vegetables with the beans. The vegetables—onion is especially good—give the beans an unexpected depth of flavor. Vegetables and beans will have about the same taste and soft texture.

Sauté the vegetables first and then add them to the cooked or nearly cooked beans. The vegetables will retain some of their original taste and texture. A variation of this is to add leftover cooked vegetables to the beans.

Simmer the vegetables with the cooking, or cooked, beans for thirty to forty minutes. The vegetables will enhance the flavor of the beans and still retain some of their individuality.

Traditionally, beans are cooked with bones, doused with fat, made meaty. But beans have also been known to get mixed up with tomatoes, sweetened with sugar or molasses, and spiced with chili. Here are some combinations and seasonings:

Soy-Sweetened Beans

This is the Japanese version of an American standby.

> *cooked soy beans with cooking water*
> *sugar, honey or molasses*
> *soy sauce   salt*

Flavor the cooked beans first with the sugar, then with the soy sauce. Add a little salt if necessary. The way I was originally shown this recipe used gobs and gobs of sugar and soy sauce. For a small side dish this candied bean is a treat, but if the beans are to be eaten in larger amounts, try seasoning them more lightly. Serve immediately, or let the sweetened beans cook for an additional half hour on top of the stove or in the oven.

Nut-Buttered Beans

This is a super-hefty, hearty, delicious dish. Again, other beans besides soy can be used.

> *cooked soy beans with cooking liquid*
> *peanut butter   salt (or soy sauce)*

If you started with a cup of dry beans, use about half a cup of peanut butter. Add a couple of tablespoons of the cooking liquid a little at a time, mixing well so that the peanut butter becomes a smooth sauce. Again this dish can be left to simmer or bake.
—Even better with sesame butter or tahini and more exotic with cashew, almond or walnut butter.

124

—This dish can be spiced up with the addition of chili powder, cumin, coriander, garlic, lemon, cardamom. Take your pick, but easy does it.

Chili Beans

Kidneys are the standard bean for this recipe, but soy, garbanzo, pinto, black-eyed peas, and others can be used.

> *cooked beans with cooking liquid   onion*
> *green pepper   tomatoes   tomato paste   chili powder*
> *salt   pepper   (garlic)   (ginger root, grated)*

Dice the onions and green peppers, then sauté them for a few minutes. Add the tomato wedges and tomato paste, along with some of the cooking liquid. Add the cooked beans and season to taste, using the garlic and ginger for additional oomph if you like them. The dish can then simmer or bake for another half hour or more.

For a milder dish, season the tomato sauce with salt, pepper, and basil, tarragon or thyme.

Blanco Beans

This is one Tassajara version of refried beans. Pintos are normally used for this recipe, but soy, kidney, garbanzo, and others are good too.

> *cooked beans with cooking liquid   onions*
> *salt   pepper   garlic   cumin seed   oregano*
> *chili   grated cheddar or jack   sour cream*

Slice and sauté the onions, using a generous amount if you like them. When the onions are golden, add some of the beans and mash them with the cooking liquid to make a creamy sauce. Do this with about half the beans, then add the remainder whole. Season with salt, pepper, garlic, ground cumin seed, oregano, and chili. Five minutes before serving, stir in the sour cream and most of the grated cheese. Let them heat gently. Garnish with the remainder of the cheese.

This dish could be baked for twenty minutes after the addition of the sour cream and cheese.

Soy Beans with Hijiki & Carrots

cooked soybeans   1 cup hijiki   2 carrots

Soak the hijiki for twenty minutes. Be sure to rinse it off after soaking (see Sea Vegetables). Squeeze out water and reserve it. Sauté in oil, then simmer in soaking liquid for thirty minutes. Add the sliced carrots to the simmering seaweed. Add the beans. It can still be seasoned to taste with sugar and soy sauce.

Five Thing Beans

soy beans   carrots   daikon   kombu   mushrooms

Cook vegies in simmering beans for thirty minutes.

Spiced Lentils

(for 4)

1 cup lentils   2½ cups water   4 cloves garlic, crushed
½ t curry   1/8 t cayenne pepper
¼ t ginger, nutmeg, coriander, or cardamom

Pressure cook one cup of dry lentils for twenty minutes with the spices. Or season cooked lentils with the same combination. When cooked, salt to taste. Add a little water if necessary.

Nuts & Seeds

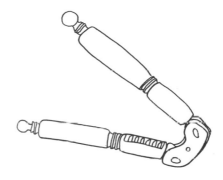

Peanuts, Almonds, Walnuts, Cashews, Brazil Nuts, Filberts; Sesame, Sunflower, Poppy Seeds

Nuts and seeds are for many people a welcome addition to many dishes. They are high in proteins, usable fats, vitamins and minerals. Raw or toasted, they enrich and decorate cooked vegetables, salads, staples and main dishes. Sometimes raw nuts are particularly tasty and interesting. Raw peanuts or sunflower seeds have something of a bean-like quality when added to cooked vegetable or grain dishes. They are also good in soups.

Nuts and seeds are frequently high priced, except when purchased unshelled or in bulk at natural food stores. Lately the price of almonds and walnuts has skyrocketed, but the price of peanuts, sunflower, and sesame seeds still makes them an excellent buy.

Any nuts or seeds, though usually peanuts, cashews or sesame seeds, can be made into a nut butter by being ground under pressure. The pressure extracts some oil from the nut meal, giving it a "buttery" texture. If the nuts or seeds are ground without pressure, oil or water can be added to give them a spreadable consistency. For hungry eaters, nut butters are a knockout heavyweight food. They can be served as a spread or diluted for sauces, drinks and soup bases.

Nuts can be chopped in a wooden bowl with a rounded chopper for use as toppings, garnishes and ingredients.

Roasted Nuts or Seeds

nuts or seeds   (salt)

The roasting can be done in a frying pan or in the oven. No oil is necessary in either case, but can be used. Put the nuts in the frying pan over a medium flame. Salt if you wish. Stir fairly frequently for even roasting. If the nuts begin to brown or burn before they are dry, turn down the heat.

For oven roasting, put the nuts on a baking sheet or in a baking pan and roast in a 350° oven for fifteen to twenty minutes. Check and stir about every five minutes. The nuts or seeds will not reach their full crunchiness until they cool.

Nut Butters

peanuts, cashews or sesame seeds   oil or water   salt

Raw or roasted nuts or seeds can be used. Grind the nuts once in a hand mill, or several times in the finest meat grinder (the latter won't work with sesame seeds). Add oil or water until the nut butter is the consistency you want.

Nut Milk

This is one way to make nuts go farther. Serve hot or cold.

nuts or seeds for grinding, or nut butters
water   honey   salt

Lightly roast and then grind the nuts or seeds. Add water gradually to the ground nuts or the nut butter until the mixture is a drinkable consistency. This can be thick like a milkshake or thinner, like milk. Sweeten to taste with honey, molasses or sugar. Does it need a pinch of salt?

Note: One-quarter cup of nuts will make nut milk out of one cup of water. If using almonds, a few drops of almond extract can be added. Otherwise a few drops of vanilla extract can be used to sweeten and flavor.

—Milk or powdered milk can be used in place of the water. The nut flavor won't be as pronounced, but the protein will be increased.

—This is also the way to go about making a nut sauce or nut soup base. The nut sauce will be thicker and possibly spiced, while the soup base will be thinner, having been mixed with bean or vegetable water.

Peanut Butter Balls

These are easy to make and can be easily varied.

1 cup peanut butter   ½ cup honey
½ cup wheat bran or wheat germ   ½ cup dry milk
½ t vanilla   1 t sugar   (sesame seeds)   (coconut)

Mix all the ingredients together. The mixture should be stiff and dry enough to shape into balls, which then may be rolled in toasted sesame seeds, coconut or chopped nuts.

—The mixture could be left whole in a block, cylinder or globe and pieces cut off as desired.

—Dried fruit, nuts, sunflower or sesame seeds could be added.

Sesame Seeds

Seeds which made "Open Sesame" magic words. They come unhulled, hulled, brown or white. There is also another variety which is black. They are expensive if purchased in little boxes from the spice shelves, cheap if purchased in bulk quantities of a pound or more. Being small and solid, they will pass through the digestive system intact unless they are ground or well chewed.

Toasted sesame seeds complement carrots, cooked greens, grains and salads. They are usually sprinkled on top. Toast seeds as you do nuts *(above)*.

Sesame Salt (Goma Shio)

At Tassajara, *goma shio* is our standard table seasoning, used particularly on cereals, grains and beans. Many people also like sesame salt with eggs and salads. Use from four to seven parts sesame seeds to one part salt.

sesame seeds   salt

Roast the sesame seeds in a frying pan or in the oven. Once they have begun to brown, add the salt and continue roasting. The seeds are ready when they can be easily crunched. Test them by taking a few out of the pan and letting them cool enough to chew on. Grind the roasted seeds and salt in a *suribachi,* a grain mill, or in a blender. The seeds should be mostly ground, but some can be left whole. The whole seeds give added flavor when bitten into. Store in a closed container when not in use. Roasted sunflower seeds, whole or ground, can be partially substituted for sesame seeds.

Tahini and Halvah:

   There are two fairly well-known sesame products, aside from sesame oils. These are *tahini* and *halvah,* which are both made from white sesame seeds. Tahini is a very creamy sesame butter and halvah is a sesame candy. Here's a recipe using tahini:

Tahini Shortbread

These cookie bars are incredibly rich and smooth. Makes one pan, 8" x 8".

¼ cup butter   1 cup tahini   ½ t salt
flour until firm (2-2½ cups)

Cream the butter with the tahini. Add the sugar, salt, and then flour until the mixture is firm, working with the hands at the last. Press the mixture into a pie tin, or square pan, about a quarter to a half inch thick. It's all right if it doesn't come all the way to the edges. Mark into pieces and cut about halfway through. An almond or walnut can be pressed on top of each piece. Bake at 325° for about forty-five minutes, or until the center is firm when gently pressed. Don't wait for it to brown—the shortbread would be overly hard, dry and crumbly.

   —Cashew butter or peanut butter could also be used.

   —A somewhat drier shortbread can be made without the butter. Much less flour (¾ to 1 cup less) will be needed.

Grains & Pasta

Brown Rice, White Rice, Wheat, Corn, Rye, Oats, Millet, Bulgur Wheat, Buckwheat

Grains are seeds, packed with just what seeds need to become plants: a germ from which the shoot will sprout and food for its growth, enveloped in protective husk and bran.

Grains are a staple food having a taste which is not really so plain, but little appreciated. Plain grains, a soothing relief from the sweet and rich, can satisfy a deep human hunger. However, people's tastes for grains vary greatly.

People say creamy smooth oatmeal is "heavenly" or "library paste." About thick oatmeal they say, "You could chew it!" or "You had to chew it!" Cornmeal mush is either their favorite or they can't stand it. Brown rice is a way of life or a poor substitute for bread. Put raisins in the cracked wheat, and you may hear, "How delicious" or "Please, no dessert with breakfast."

Whole grains take a generous amount of cooking and chewing to be eaten. Unchewed whole grains are not digested. Because of the lengthy cooking and chewing involved in eating uncracked grains, they aren't often prepared that way. In fact, rice, millet, barley and buckwheat are the only grains which are suitable for cooking whole, and of these, buckwheat isn't really a grain (grass seed); it is related to dock and rhubarb, which helps explain why it isn't as tough as the others.

Cooking Whole Grains

Amounts: One cup dry whole grain, when cooked, serves two hungry grain-eaters or up to six people eating amply of other foods. So usually one cup dry serves three to five.

Washing the grain: Rinse the grain once in cold water. Stir the water and grain around with your hands to gently loosen the dust and small bits of dirt. Pour out the rinse water through a strainer. If the water appears dirty, rinse again.

Preparing the pot: Rub oil around the inside of the cooking pot, both the bottom and sides. Do this for all grain and cereal dishes. The grain is less likely to stick and the pot will be much easier to clean.

Basic Ways to Cook Grains

Although the ratio of water to grain and the length of cooking time varies, there are two basic ways for cooking whole or cracked grains. In the first, the grain is combined with cold water, while in the second, the grain is combined with boiling water.

I.

The cold water method: Put the cleaned grain in the greased pot along with salt and water. Cover, bring to a boil (the steam will be escaping from around the sides of the lid), then reduce to a simmer for the duration of the cooking time. Try not to look in, as precious steam will escape. Listen to the sounds and sniff the air to determine how the cooking is proceeding. When all the water is absorbed, there will no longer be a bubbling sound, but more of a popping or crackling, the sound of the grain toasting—you should be able to smell it—on the bottom of the pan. It is proper for the grain to brown slightly, but it's done before you smell it burning. Open the pot and stir up the grain so that the drier kernels on top are mixed with the wetter ones on the bottom. Cover and let stand a few minutes before serving.

II.

The boiling water method: This method starts with hot water and often with hot grain. Start the water heating and in the meantime sauté the grain, either with or without oil. Oil (or butter) adds flavor and calories. Continue the sautéing to whatever shade of brown you prefer. (The toasting process develops the flavor but destroys vitamins.) Either add the grain to water boiling in a cereal pot, or do the sautéing in the pot, remove it briefly from the flame and then pour in the boiling water. Use hotpads for this and watch out for the steam. For whole grains cover the pot immediately after the water is added. Since the grain cooks some when sautéed, slightly less water is necessary to complete the cooking when this method is used.

Brown Rice

Boiled

(Serves 3-5)

rice   water   salt

Use twice as much water as rice, and a quarter teaspoon salt for every cup of rice. Continue as above.

Pressure Cooked Brown Rice

This makes the rice so tasty and easy to chew that people usually eat more of it than when it is just plain boiled.

rice   for every cup of rice, 1-3/8 cups water
¼ t salt per cup of rice

Wash rice. Place all ingredients in pressure cooker. Cover and heat to boiling. Cook over low heat for thirty minutes. Then bring to 15 lb. pressure and cook for twenty minutes more. Remove from the heat and allow to depressurize completely on its own. If necessary, the pressure cooker can be cooled by running cold water over the top. Remove cover and stir thoroughly. Replace cover without jiggler and allow to sit five to fifteen minutes before serving.

White Rice

white rice   water   (salt)

Use between one and a quarter and one and a third cups of water for every cup of rice. White rice usually comes coated with talc. The talc is not appetizing to bugs and rodents and it's not too good for people either, so the rice needs to be thoroughly rinsed off. It takes three to five rinsings to remove most of the talc. The rinse water should be nearly clear after the final rinsing.

The Japanese cook their rice without salt, but a quarter teaspoon per cup of rice could be added. Cook the same as for boiled brown rice, except that it will take only about twenty minutes of simmering. Be sure to bring the water to a vigorous boil before turning down to a simmer. All with the lid on. When cooking is finished, open, stir and fluff. Then let sit with the lid on.

Parsley Rice

Even in hot weather this rice looks cool and delicious.

cooked white rice   minced parsley

Mix a generous amount of minced parsley with the cooked white rice so that it is well greened. Serve with butter, salt and pepper.

—This could also be made with Bulgur wheat, brown rice, buttered noodles or spaghetti.

Whole Barley

Prepare this like brown rice, either boiling or pressure cooking. Whole barley has a rather pleasant chewiness. By itself it is a heavy dish, but its flavor and texture make it an excellent addition to bean dishes, stuffings and soups.

Whole Barley with White Rice

barley   white rice   water

Use about three parts of white rice to one part barley. Cook the barley as usual. Proceed with the standard white rice recipe, combining cooked barley with the uncooked rice and water.

—This recipe can also be done with whole wheat berries. Whole wheat berries are extremely chewy and need even more lengthy cooking than barley or brown rice, but the procedure is the same.

—Or use buckwheat, which will cook in the same length of time as the rice.

Millet & Buckwheat Groats

Both of these can be prepared by either of the two basic methods, although most people prefer them sautéed first. Use one part grain to two parts water, with a quarter teaspoon of salt per cup of grain. Again one cup grain to start with serves three to five, depending on the rest of the menu.

Prepared by the first method, allow twenty minutes cooking time. If sautéed first, simmer for ten to fifteen minutes after adding the boiling water.

Bulgur Wheat

Bulgur wheat is wheat which has been cracked, steamed and toasted, so it is in a sense precooked. It is included here with the uncracked grains, since it is most frequently prepared as a dinner dish rather than a breakfast cereal.

*one part bulgur wheat to one and a third
or one and a half parts water*

Sauté first, then boil. Cook like White Rice, or like Cereal (p. 138).

135

Grains with Vegetables

More elaborate dishes will be considered in the main dish section. For now, let's look at simple grain/vegetable combinations. Onions are utilized most frequently because they add another flavor dimension. Celery, green peppers, carrots are often used in combination with onion.

Onions & Grain

1 cup grain   2 cups water   ¼ t salt   ½-1 onion

Dice the onion. Sauté it in the grain-cooking pot for several minutes. Remove the onion, add a little more oil and roast the grain for five minutes. Stir in the onions, salt, and add the boiling water. Cover and simmer until well done.

—Do the same with celery, green pepper or carrot.
—Thyme, basil and garlic can be used to season this dish.
—Cooked vegetables could also be stirred into the grain when it has finished cooking.
—Grain dishes may be garnished with grated cheese or chopped nuts.

Refried Grains

The grain is completely cooked, then added to sautéed vegetables and fried—an excellent way to use leftover cooked grains, or vegetables for that matter.

cooked grain   onion, celery, carrot, peppers
egg   soy sauce   green onions

Not all of these vegetables need be used, maybe just onion and one other. Cut the vegetables into small pieces and stir-fry for four to five minutes. Break up the grain and mix it with the vegetables. Continue frying while stirring and scraping the bottom of the pan. When the grain is heated through, season with salt, pepper, soy sauce. Make a space in the center, drop in an egg or two, and quickly stir in with the grain. Garnish with finely sliced green onions, nuts or grated cheese.

—Other seasonings could be used: garlic, ginger, thyme, hot peppers or curry.

—Other leftover cooked vegetables could be used. Cut them up if necessary and add with the cooked grain.

—For another style of refried grain, use raisins, nuts, diced apple or toasted sunflower seeds.

Grain Soups

Whole grains can be made more soupy with the addition of extra water. They make a flavorful broth.

1 cup grain: rice, barley, buckwheat, cracked wheat
4 cups water   ¼ t salt

Oil the pot around the sides and bottom. Roast the grain in a little oil if desired. Add salt and water, bring to boiling, then simmer for forty to sixty minutes or longer. White rice cooked this way makes a thick, creamy soup base. (For more about grain soups, see Soups.)

Cereals

Grains go through a mill to have their hulls removed. This hulling removes the outermost layer of bran, which is also known as the chaff. Polishing a grain removes further layers of bran. Hulled grain is milled into cereal or flour. Cereals are coarser, with distinct pieces of "meal," while flours have been completely ground into powder. Once grains are broken up or ground in this way, water enters more readily, cooking time is reduced, and chewing is made less arduous.

Some grains, especially oats, are rolled, which means they are flattened between rollers. Oatmeal is usually rolled and then further broken up and processed.

Grains milled for cereal are often known as "creams": cream of wheat, cream of rice, etc. Flour can also be used to make a very creamy cereal.

137

Cooking Cereals

Cereals can be cooked by either of the two processes already described for cooking grains. For cooking cereal a thick-bottomed pot is preferable, since the mush tends to burn on the bottom otherwise. Cereal cooked in a thin-bottomed pot needs more stirring and a very low flame. In either case oil the sides and bottom of the pot before adding the cereal and water.

Basic Hot Cereal Recipe

(Serves 4)

> *3½ cups water   ¼ t salt   1-2 T oil or butter*
> *1 cup cereal: rice cream, barley cream, cracked wheat,*
> *rye meal, steel cut oats, corn meal, millet meal,*
> *bulgur wheat, buckwheat cream,*
> *or 1½ cups oatmeal or rolled oats*

Start the water heating in a separate pot, while the cereal is being sautéed in the cereal pot. Stir the roasting cereal for even browning, until a pleasing grain aroma greets your nose. Take the pot off the fire, let it sit a minute or two, and then pour into the boiling or nearly boiling water. Use hotpads! Stir briskly, then return to *low flame* and continue cooking for ten to thirty minutes. If the cereal is burning, continue the cooking in a double boiler. Add a little more hot water if the cereal gets too thick.

Variations and Additions:
   —Do the whole process using the first method for uncracked grain. Put all the ingredients in a pot and heat to boiling, then turn down to simmer until ready.
   —Add leftover cooked grains or cereals to the water at the start: brown rice in oatmeal, Bulgur wheat in cracked wheat, corn kernels in corn meal, and so forth.
   —For an even wheatier cracked wheat cereal, add either plain or toasted wheat germ just before the end of cooking.
   —Add dry milk powder, toasted sunflower seeds, chopped nuts, nut butters, five to ten minutes before the end of cooking.
   —Add raisins, chopped dates, sliced figs or other dried fruits

five minutes or more before the end of cooking.

One suggestion about adding things: Find out if everyone likes it that way. I like each thing separate, so that I can go from one to the other. Served separately, stewed fruit and nuts can be mixed with the cereal or not.

Pasta

Pasta is, for many people, a favorite way of eating grain. Spaghetti, noodles, macaroni, lasagne; the assortment of shapes and sizes is remarkable. The versatility of pasta is easily forgotten. Aside from being served with the usual sauces, pasta is also excellent in casseroles, soups, sometimes salads as well.

For cooking noodles, spaghetti, lasagne, macaroni, the directions are on the package, aren't they? One pound serves four or five, generally.

> *large pot of boiling water   salt   oil   olive oil (butter)*
> *pasta: noodles, spaghetti, lasagne, macaroni, fettucini, etc.*
> *salt   pepper   herbs*

Start the water heating, add some salt and a few tablespoons of oil, which helps keep the pasta from sticking together. When the water is boiling, fan in the noodles or spaghetti so that they can separate somewhat. Bring the water back to a boil, then reduce the heat so that the water is just boiling.

There is, of course, the eight-minute method for determining when pasta is done, but there are some other possibilities, too. Some famous restaurants have a spaghetti range—an empty wall or ceiling which a string of spaghetti can be tossed at. If it sticks to the wall it's done; if not, keep cooking. Many people cook spaghetti *"al dente"*—biting a piece between two front teeth to test for proper texture.

When cooked, drain the pasta and save the cooking liquid as you would when cooking vegetables. If you let the pasta sit at this point, it will tend to lump together, so I like to toss it with a little butter or (olive) oil right away, then let it sit above hot water if it's not to be served until later. Season with salt and pepper and crushed basil.

139

Fried Noodles

With Daikon and Turnip

noodles, boiling water   daikon   turnip
soy sauce   salt   oil

Fan the noodles into the boiling salted water. Remove when tender, but still slightly hard. Drain in colander, reserving the water for soup. Cut the vegetables in matchstick pieces and sauté for three to four minutes. Add the noodles and soy sauce. Cook an additional two or three minutes.

—Try other vegetables: onion, celery, green pepper, carrot and apple are tasty. May be garnished with chopped parsley or sliced green onions.

Here's another way with fried noodles:

noodles   carrots   hijiki seaweed (or onion)
parsley   sage   cumin seed

Wash and soak the hijiki (p. 106). Cook the noodles until the water returns to a fast boil. Remove and drain. Cut up the carrots and steam in a frying pan with water until done, adding the parsley and cumin seed. Put in the salt and hijiki, along with the noodles. Fry in a small amount of oil. Add the carrots when the noodles are thoroughly heated.

Dairy Products

Milk, Buttermilk, Butter, Margarine, Cream, Sour Cream, Cream Cheese (Neufchatel), Cottage Cheese, Cheeses, Yogurt

While some people are able to sustain themselves without milk products, for others they are what makes a vegetarian diet possible and enjoyable—milk on cereal and berries, grilled cheese sandwiches, cottage cheese salads, cheesecake and whipped cream. Milk turns up throughout the day and throughout the menu in dressings, sauces, soups, spreads and desserts.

Short Cooking, Moderate Heat:

As a rule, milk products need very little cooking. They tend to brown or burn easily and they frequently curdle (or separate) with heat. The smell of burnt milk is extremely pervasive and not at all appetizing, so be sure to heat or cook with a moderate flame. Milk will tend to burn before it gets to the boiling point, and even in recipes which call for boiling, it needn't really be that hot.

Butter also will burn if it is heated to the same temperatures to which oils are heated for sautéing. Used together with a regular cooking oil, butter can be heated to a higher temperature. Otherwise, cook more slowly when using butter.

Cheese does not need cooking. Once melted, it begins to get tough and stringy with further cooking.

Cottage Cheese

This has unexpected versatility and is one of our favorite foods.

Cottage Cheese Salad

cottage cheese   apple   orange   banana   pear
raisins   sunflower seeds   walnuts
lemon juice   honey (or sugar)   salt

Dice all the fruit and mix with the nuts and seeds. Season with lemon juice, salt, and sweetening. Add the cottage cheese. This salad can be made more creamy with the addition of sour cream or mayonnaise.

Variations:
  —This dish has been a hit with just roasted peanuts added to the cottage cheese.
  —It can also be made with vegetables instead of, or possibly in addition to, fruits. Use diced carrots, onion, (green onion,) green pepper, celery, minced parsley, with lemon juice and possibly raisins and nuts. Tomato wedges could also be mixed in or used to decorate the top.
  —A simple recipe would be to add minced parsley, green onion, olives. Sprinkle with paprika.
  —Add some bleu cheese for flavor.

Hot Cottage Cheese

This is a soft, soothing dish which can also be used as a stuffing.

cottage cheese   onions   green peppers   (mushrooms)
eggs   salt, pepper   (paprika)

Slice or dice the onions and green peppers, then sauté them in oil. Mix in the cottage cheese and season with salt and pepper. Add two or three eggs for every half pound of cottage cheese. Heat this gently on top of the stove or bake at 325° for fifteen to twenty minutes. Sprinkle generously with the paprika before or after cooking. Sautéed mushrooms could also be added, as well as most other vegetables (first cook them until nearly done).

—Using a lot of vegetables makes this dish *"Vegetables with Cheese,"* whereas fewer vegetables makes it *"Hot Cottage Cheese with Vegetables."*

Cottage Cheese Sauce

Thinned, the above recipe is one way to use cottage cheese as a sauce. It could also be added to flour based milk sauces, or mixed with sour cream or yogurt, and be gently heated. High heat will cause cottage cheese to separate.

Some people find the curds in cottage cheese objectionable in sauces. To remedy this the cottage cheese can be sieved or blended. Also available is a whipped cottage cheese which makes an instant vegetable sauce or salad dressing with a minimum of added seasonings.

Cottage Cheese Dessert

cottage cheese   honey   vanilla
nutmeg   (nuts, fruits, dried fruits)

Sweeten and season to taste. (Sweetness is emphasized with vanilla and nutmeg.) Garnish with nuts, fruits or dried fruits. May also be sweetened or decorated with fruit jams or jellies.

Note: Adding eggs and baking (with a crust) makes this recipe cottage cheesecake.

Ricotta Cheese

This is another inexpensive, soft milk cheese, similar to cottage cheese. But ricotta has a smoother consistency. It can be used in place of cottage cheese in any of the preceding recipes.

Ricotta Dessert

ricotta   strawberries   raisins
bananas   maple syrup

A mound of ricotta in the center of a dessert dish. Encircle with the fruit and pour maple syrup over the top.

Sour Cream

An instant sauce for vegetables, salads, potatoes, noodles—sour cream is also used in several soups—beet, carrot, yam—to offset their sweetness. Yogurt can replace sour cream, not in terms of calories, but in terms of protein, tartness, moisture.

Cheese

We use mostly cheddar, Monterey Jack and Swiss, and lesser amounts of Parmesan, Fontinella and others. Many recipes using cheese appear in other sections of this book. If a meal seems to lack substance or character, cheese is often found to be the answer. It can go into vegetable, grain, bean and egg dishes, soups, sauces and salads. Here are a few recipes not mentioned in the other sections.

Cheese Sandwich

This is our standard, day-off bag lunch sandwich. All the ingredients are put out after breakfast and everyone makes his own.

bread   (butter)   cheese slices
lettuce or alfalfa sprouts   tomato slices   onion slices
pickle (in the sandwich or on the side)
mustard   mayonnaise

Assemble as you will, using the ingredients which you want. Ricotta cheese or sour cream can also be used for a spread. Too much? Some people put in even more things: avocado, cucumber, sunflower seeds. Well, assemble as you will.

Grilled Cheese Sandwiches

Once again the possibilities are endless. Here are three basic ways of making an open-faced grilled cheese sandwich.

I.

parsley, chives or green onion
cheese: cheddar, jack, swiss or other cheese
vegetables: choice of tomato, sprouts, olives,
lettuce, avocado, mushrooms
toast

Toast one or two sides of the bread. Arrange the vegetables on top —the tomato and mushroom could be briefly sautéed beforehand. Put the cheese, sliced or grated, on top of the vegetables. Broil to melt the cheese. Garnish with parsley, chives or sliced green onion.

II.

vegetable: radish rounds, green pepper strips,
celery slices, onion rings, tomato rounds
cheese   toast

Put the cheese slices on the toast and decorate with a variety of vegetable slices. Broil until cheese melts.

III.

vegetables: choice of onion, mushroom,
celery, green pepper, etc.
soft cheese: cream, neufchatel, cottage,
or ricotta (bleu cheese added)
toast

Spread the toast with a soft cheese, possibly mixed with bleu cheese for added flavor. Smother top with sautéed vegetables. Grill to heat.

Additional comments: These three methods can be combined in various ways. For instance, a soft cheese could be spread on the toast before the vegetables in the first recipe.

Any of these recipes can be seasoned: Garlic salt, sweet basil, marjoram, oregano, thyme, can be sprinkled on the vegetables or cheese, as well as simply salt and pepper.

—Other spices can be used, such as nutmeg, mace, ground ginger, dry mustard, cumin and curry powder. These spices are very strong, so use them sparingly.

Closed-Faced Grilled Cheese Sandwich

bread   cheese   butter or oil

Butter the outside surfaces of the bread and put the cheese in between. Fry over medium-low heat in a covered frying pan. Herbs and other seasonings could be used just as in the open-face sandwiches.

Cheese with Fruit

Dessert or snack. This is just another reminder that cheese goes this way too.

fruit: apples, pears, grapes, oranges, other
cheese: cheddar, jack, swiss, provolone,
edam, gouda, (cream cheese ball,) other

Cut the cheese in slices, sticks or wedges. Serve the fruit whole with knives for slicing at the table, or pre-slice the fruit. Apple is good with any cheese. If in doubt, taste-test various combinations. A glass of wine?

Cream Cheese (Neufchatel)

This versatile cheese product can be used straight as a spread, thinned as a sauce, or to replace cream in cooking. It is rich in both protein and calories. Neufchatel is made in the same way as cream cheese, but with milk in place of cream. It has fewer calories per whatever. Here is one way to use these cheeses— there are others elsewhere in the book:

Cream Cheese Ball or Log

The cream cheese holds the other cheeses and seasonings together.

cream cheese   grated cheese (whatever kind you have)
(bleu cheese)   milk   toasted sesame seeds
salt   pepper   garlic   dry mustard
green onion   parsley   herbs
(or use: garlic   onion or celery salt)

Work the cream cheese until it is creamy. Mix in bleu cheese and one or more kinds of grated cheese for flavoring. Add a small amount of milk if the mixture gets too thick. Season to taste. Shape into a ball, or balls, or a log, and roll in the toasted sesame seeds.

For *Dessert Cream Cheese Balls,* mix raisins, nuts, chopped dates, lemon or orange peel with the softened cream cheese. Season with vanilla extract and cinnamon. To use as a topping, thin the mixture with sour cream or yogurt. Modify or eliminate seasoning depending on what is to be topped: pancakes, vegetables, salads, grains, grilled cheese sandwiches. It could be heated in a double boiler or over gentle heat. Do not boil, or the mixture will separate.

Yogurt

This is a cultured milk product, which is easier than milk to digest, and which contains beneficial bacteria that can produce B vitamins in the intestines.

How to Make Yogurt:
   The bacteria in yogurt grow in milk and cause the milk to thicken over a period of three to eight hours. As a part of their life processes,

they convert milk sugar into lactic acid. The basic process for making yogurt is to introduce yogurt bacteria into some warm milk and keep that milk warm for several hours until it thickens.

To grow, the yogurt-making bacteria need milk which is at a hospitable temperature, 90° to 120°, or most appropriately 105° to 110° (barely warm on your wrist). At higher temperatures these bacteria are destroyed and at lower temperatures they do not grow well, but other bacteria will. Sometimes the milk is first heated to 180° to kill unwanted bacteria, then cooled to yogurt-making temperature.

For yogurt bacteria starter, use any fresh, plain yogurt. To start the first batch of homemade yogurt, buy a small amount of good-quality plain yogurt at a market. Buy one that you like, since the starter will produce yogurt of a similar flavor. After you've made the first batch you can, of course, use some of it to start the second.

What milk to use? We use mostly dry milk to make our yogurt, twice as much as is normally used to make milk for drinking. Concentrated (not evaporated) milk also makes an excellent creamy yogurt, diluted one to one instead of one to two.

How to keep the yogurt-milk warm until it thickens? There are several ways to do this. The yogurt-cultured milk is kept in covered bottles or pots. These bottles or pots should be thoroughly cleaned and preheated. One way to keep them warm is to place them in warm water over a pilot light on top of the stove, or in the oven. No pilot light? Another way is to heat the oven to 350° for about five minutes, then turn it off and put the yogurt in, padded with towels. If the oven cools off too much, turn it on for a couple of minutes every hour or two. Often a 75-watt light bulb will keep an oven, or a cardboard box, warm enough to culture yogurt. Get a cord with a socket on the end of it, cut a circular hole just large enough for the socket to fit in the side of the box. When it is in place, screw the light bulb in from the inside. If using the light bulb in an oven, the oven door should have a good spring, or it may not close well. One more method is to wrap warm milk bottles with towels and put them in a styrofoam ice chest.

Yogurt Recipes

I.

4 cups water, at about 115°-120°
2½-3 cups dry milk   1-2 T yogurt*

Mix the water and powdered milk thoroughly together. The mixture should be at about 110°. Mix a few tablespoons of this with the yogurt, then pour the thinned yogurt back into the milk. If not already in a clean preheated bottle or pot, pour the mixture into same and cover. Set it in the warmed space you have devised for it (see above). Check in three hours, and periodically thereafter. When it has begun to thicken, refrigerate it.

*The more yogurt used for starter, the tarter the new batch of yogurt will be.

II.

1 quart concentrated milk
1 quart boiling water
3 T yogurt

Mix the boiling water with the concentrated milk. When it has cooled to 115° (slightly warm on your wrist), mix a few tablespoons with the yogurt, then mix this back into the milk. Pour into a cleaned, preheated container, cover, and set in a warm home until the mixture begins to thicken. Refrigerate.

III.

1 quart whole or skim milk   4 t yogurt

Heat the milk gently to 180° (little bubbles forming around the sides and bottom of the pot). Pour into the cleaned bottle(s) and let cool to 110°. Mix a little of the warm milk with the yogurt, then divide this mixture evenly among the bottles. Cover and put in a warm place. Refrigerate when it begins to thicken.

Yogurt should thicken completely in, at most, eight hours. Failure can result from the milk being too hot when the yogurt was added, the mixture not being kept warm enough, the yogurt starter being defective, or antibiotics being present in the milk. You can try again with the same batch of milk if you heat it slowly to 180° to kill any foreign bacteria, cool to 110°, add some more yogurt and start over again.

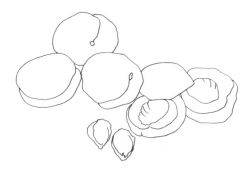

Eggs

The protein in eggs comes closer to being completely utilizable by the body than that of any other single food. Eggs are extremely versatile and, for many people, nearly indispensable, due both to their high nutritional value and to the fact that they can be cooked in so many different ways. Eggs can be fried, poached, scrambled, boiled or baked. They can also be added to salads, salad dressings, soups, sauces, casseroles and desserts. Eggs carry the oil of mayonnaise and the butter of hollandaise.

As a rule, eggs are cooked with moderate heat, so that they will be tender rather than leathery. When heated too fast in a sauce or soup, eggs will scramble rather than thickening and enriching. If the heat is too high for a custard or meringue, the egg will harden and "weep" water.

The Fried Egg

Sunny side up, over easy, glorious.

If you like your eggs lacy brown, you probably already know how to get them to come out that way. The main difficulty with fried eggs is getting the top of the white cooked without the white becoming leathery and the yolk becoming solid. Start with a moderately hot pan, so that when the egg goes in there is not a great sizzle and the white doesn't bubble—it just gradually turns white. Here are two methods:

151

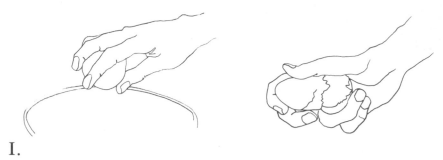

I.

eggs   butter or oil

Put a generous amount of oil or butter in a moderately heated frying pan. Put in the eggs. If you're cooking more than one egg and you want them done at the same time, break them into a bowl first, then slide them gently into the frying pan together—they can be cut apart later. As they cook, spoon butter or oil on top of them to cook the upper surface. These eggs can also go over easy when they are firm, flipping them boy-scout fashion with the pan, or using a spatula. Leave very briefly (half a minute possibly), then flop back and serve.

II.

This is the combination fry-steam method.

eggs   butter or oil   water or stock   (lid or cover)

Use a modest amount of oil or butter in the moderately heated frying pan. After eggs are in, add a couple of tablespoons of water, and cover the pan. Leave on moderate heat. Steam from the water will cook the top of the eggs. Give them a couple of minutes, then take a peek. The white should be all cooked and the yolk glazed, but still runny.

—The water can be stock for added flavor, compliments or controversy. Pink eggs with tomato juice! "Can't we just have eggs sometimes?"

—Strips of cheese can be put on top of the frying eggs before the pan is covered.

—If these fried eggs are done on a griddle, an inverted baking pan can serve as a lid.

—If you like them, fried eggs make an excellent topping for grain and bean dishes.

Poached Eggs

At best these eggs are tender, plump and juicy. Not without reason are they the eggs of Benedict. A warning: they can be a headache. Have all of your tools ready.

> eggs   water or stock   vinegar   salt
> dish towel or sponge   rubber spatula
> perforated spoon (if available)

The eggs are cooked in water. Have at least a cup of water per egg, and for every cup add about ½ teaspoon of vinegar and ½ teaspoon of salt. The vinegar is to help keep the egg from spreading out once it's broken into the water.

Heat water, vinegar and salt to boiling, then turn heat down to medium low. As soon as the boiling stops, start putting in the eggs, depositing them at the surface as much as possible, rather than splashing them into the water. They should spread a bit, but not all over the place. Let them cook slowly for a minute or so, and then gently loosen the eggs from the pan bottom with a rubber spatula. Cook another two or three minutes, until they can be lifted from the water without breaking. Try picking them up with the perforated spoon, and if solid enough, remove from the water, then rest the spoon on the folded up dish towel or clean sponge to allow the excess water to be absorbed. Remove from spoon to a heated platter. When all the eggs are on the platter, more water can be absorbed by tilting the platter slightly, and mopping up the water with a paper towel.

—Eggs can be cooked this way in soups a few minutes before they are to be served. In that case allow an egg per person, with possibly an extra one for breakage.

Boiled Eggs

Soft: Sometimes vinegar is added to the water to keep the egg from spreading if there happens to be a crack in the shell.

eggs in shell   water   (vinegar)

Bring water to a boil, turn down to simmering. Put in the eggs for four minutes. Remove and drain. Run cold water over the eggs briefly to stop the cooking.

Hard:

eggs   water   (vinegar)

Put the eggs in cold water with vinegar. Heat to boiling, then simmer for ten minutes. Drain off hot water and add cold water to stop the cooking. Putting the eggs in cold water will also make them easier to peel.

Scrambled Eggs

Again, these are best cooked with moderate heat. Some people like their scrambled eggs completely dry, but most people seem to prefer them slightly moist. The eggs go on cooking even when the frying pan is removed from the flame, so for moist eggs remove the pan from the fire well before they are done.

eggs   salt, pepper   milk   oil or butter

Beat the eggs and season them with salt and pepper. Add a little milk (a tablespoon or so per egg) if you like. Cook in a well-oiled moderately hot pan, stirring frequently, and scraping the cooked egg off the sides and bottom of the pan. If you want them smooth, whip with a wire whisk before serving.

Omelettes

Adding Vegetables to Omelettes or Scrambled Eggs:
   Except for very tender vegetables such as tomatoes, avocados, sprouts and possibly squashes, I prefer to sauté the vegetables

before adding them to the eggs. Slice or dice any vegetables you happen to like or have on hand and then sauté them. If making scrambled eggs, add the beaten seasoned eggs to the vegetables and continue cooking as in the scrambled egg recipe. Omelettes can be made with vegetables this same way, but I prefer to remove the sautéed vegetables from the frying pan and then get the eggs started on their own—in fresh oil if necessary. I find this especially helpful for developing the "skin" in method I, and for readily beating the eggs in method III. Leaving the vegetables in the pan and adding the eggs works best for omelette method II.

Adding Cheese to Omelettes or Scrambled Eggs:

Cheese doesn't need cooking, just melting, so add it towards the end of the cooking. Any grated or dried cheese can be used inside, and cheese in strips or slices can be artfully arranged on top of the omelette.

Cream cheese or neufchatel, cottage cheese or ricotta can also be used. These make eggs wonderfully soft and creamy.

Omelettes with milk or cottage cheese in them won't become runny if cooked slowly. Faster cooking makes the whey separate out of the milk or cottage cheese.

Omelettes are usually folded in half towards the end of their cooking, so that the cheese and vegetables inside heat thoroughly. It also makes the filling a surprise.

Especially if the omelette is being served for dinner, accompany it with a sauce: either plain white, brown, mushroom or cheese (see Sauces).

Here are three methods for cooking omelettes:

I.

The No-Stir Method

> *eggs   salt, pepper   oil or butter*

Beat the eggs and season them with salt and pepper. Cook in a well-oiled moderately hot pan. When the eggs are poured in a "skin" should form right away on the sides and bottom. Let the eggs cook slowly without stirring for a couple of minutes, so that the skin thickens considerably. Lift the edges of the thickened

155

egg and tilt the pan so that the liquid egg runs underneath. Repeat this process of cooking, lifting, tilting as necessary to complete the cooking of the omelette.

II.

Whipped White, Oven Finished

> eggs, separated   salt, pepper   oil or butter
> oven-proof frying pan

Separate the eggs and whip the whites to soft peaks. Beat the yolks and fold them into the whites along with the seasoning. Start the eggs cooking in a well-oiled pan over moderate heat. After the bottom is cooked (five to eight minutes?), put the eggs in a moderate oven (350°) or under a moderate broiler to finish the cooking.

The oven-baked omelette won't fold over, so arrange a design of vegetables and cheese on top before putting it into the oven.

III.

The Constant Stir Method

> eggs, beaten   salt, pepper   oil or butter
> wire whisk or egg beater

This method makes exceptional eggs. Pour the seasoned beaten eggs into a well-oiled slightly heated pan, and do the cooking over low to moderate flame. Stir continuously with a wire whisk. The eggs are meant to thicken gradually without scrambling. When they have gotten quite thick, so that there is a deep furrow following the whisk around, stop stirring and turn the heat up, let cook briefly so that the omelette sets.

Seasonings for Omelettes or Scrambled Eggs:
   —One of the best ways we've found to season eggs is with soy sauce replacing the salt.

—Herbs to try with eggs include thyme, basil, tarragon, marjoram, oregano. Other seasonings to use in moderate amounts include garlic, curry powder, chili, ginger, nutmeg.

Egg Salad

3 eggs, hard boiled   cottage cheese   yogurt
salt   pepper

Shell and cut up the hard-boiled eggs. For every egg add about a third of a cup of cottage cheese and moisten this mixture with a few tablespoons of yogurt. Season with salt and pepper, a pinch of curry. Some paprika?

Super Egg Nog

This is a warm milk drink which we used to have for breakfast sometimes.

4 cups milk   2 eggs
1 T white sugar   ½ t vanilla extract   (nutmeg)

Heat the milk, but do not boil (it burns very easily). Beat the eggs, and beat in one cup of the heated milk, gradually. Add the egg-milk mixture to the rest of the heated milk. Stir in the vanilla and the sugar. Sprinkle nutmeg on top, if you like it.

Pumpkin
Isn't Always Pie

Pumpkin isn't always pie.
Potato isn't always salad.
Food is what we make it.
Food is how we take it.

Rice, sometimes a pudding, could be a salad.
Carrot salad could go in a pilaf casserole.
Gazpacho, a liquid salad, is called a soup.
Out of context the familiar can be intriguing.
Put in context the unfamiliar can be swallowed.
Dress it up, thin it out, season, garnish,
or perhaps do nothing, almost nothing.

Up to now emphasis has been put on preparing things simply, preparing things so that we can enjoy their unique spirit. Now let's consider how things can be mixed together, and still retain this spirit.

Plainness can accentuate complexity, and fanciness can make plainness deeply refreshing.

A strong flavor, texture, or color may overpower a weak one, but also one flavor, texture, or color may bring out the qualities of other ingredients, sometimes by sameness, sometimes by contrast. Within the same dish, or among several dishes, work at developing complementary relationships.

By mixing things together we make various interesting dishes; soups, salads, main courses. However, adding or mixing ingredients will not automatically make a dish interesting or superior. Try simpler combinations first and then elaborate. The more ingredients that are involved, the more everything tends to take on a uniform drabness. Not that it is impossible to make a good dish with numerous ingredients, but that it is more difficult, so some caution is necessary. The same is true of seasonings, which easily overpower every other taste.

Food is food only if it is eaten, so we make things that the people we are cooking for can relish and enjoy.

"Man has never taken kindly to having his eating habits changed or reformed." —H. Bieler

Salads & Salad Dressings

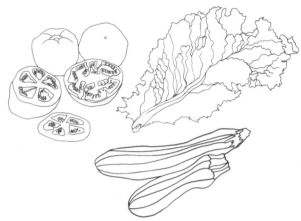

something to start on
side or main dish
something to end with

Salads are meant to be refreshing—in appearance, taste, and feeling. A refreshing change from the hot, heavy, soft, and dry. The vegetable chapter includes many suggestions for how to serve vegetables as salads, and the lettuce section includes several kinds of simple dressings, along with guidelines for the care of lettuce. Here salad making in general is discussed, as well as many dressings including basic oil and vinegar dressing.

Outline for Making Salads

Background Ingredients:
    lettuce, cabbage, carrots, spinach, cucumber, cauliflower, broccoli, potatoes, sprouts, beets, tomatoes, green beans, asparagus, other?
    beans: kidney, lentil, garbanzo, other?
    grains: rice, bulgur wheat, other?

160

The ingredient upon which a particular salad is based is the "Background," which is how the salad gets its name, for instance, "Potato Salad."

Foreground Ingredients:
    *green, yellow or purple onions, celery, green peppers, red
    radishes, capers, dill or sweet pickles, olives, cheese, nuts,
    seeds, fruit and dried fruit*

These are employed to complement each other and the basic ingredient, adding color, shape, taste, zest. The ingredients listed under "Background" could also be used in lesser amounts as "Foreground" ingredients.

If a salad is kept fairly simple, say three or five ingredients, each ingredient can have some prominence, but it is also intriguing to "hide" ingredients in a salad. Consider how to cut each thing. How does it look? How well does it taste when bitten into? Can it be easily chewed? Does it need cooking?

Consider how to arrange the ingredients: Mixed together? Separate rows? Circles? Layers? Dressing in the middle surrounded by the salad ingredients? If each ingredient to be used is kept in a separate bowl, some of them may be arranged decoratively on top of the salad rather than being mixed in.

Garnishings:
    *croutons, toasted sunflower seeds and raisins, poppy seeds,
    toasted sesame seeds, grated cheese, parsley, watercress*

Most of the Background or Foreground ingredients are suitable for use as garnishings also.

Choice of Salad Dressing:
    Feel out the dressing: Just salt? Oil and vinegar? Better with some creaminess? Mild or hot? Wet and tangy? More sour? Sweet?
    Jump right in and make yourself a salad, or take a look at the suggestions and specific recipe combinations which follow.

Lettuce Salads

These can be made with just one kind of lettuce or with a combination of lettuces, and possibly with spinach, watercress, nasturtium leaves. Choose a simple dressing from the Lettuce section (p. 71), or a dressing from the following section. To maintain the freshness of the greens, the dressing should be applied just before serving. For the same reason, ingredients such as tomatoes and juicy fruits should not be combined with the lettuce until the last minute (or five).

Salads are *tossed* so that the dressing which has settled to the bottom of the bowl is brought to the top and mixed with the ingredients. Toss thoroughly so that all the dressing is used—no puddle on the bottom of the bowl.

Here are suggested foreground ingredients to use with a background of lettuce:

> *tomato wedges and avocado strips; shredded red cabbage and sprouts, tomato wedges and cheddar cheese chunks; strips of broccoli core and grated carrot, sliced oranges and raisins; sliced radishes, green pepper, mushrooms and parsley; carrot, celery, tomato, roasted almonds; cucumber and grated cooked beets; cantaloupe strips and sliced radishes; leftover vegetables, cut into salad pieces; sliced orange, carrot, celery, and walnuts*

Cabbage Salads

Here are some excellent salads using cabbage for a background:

Chunks & Pieces

Shredded cabbage with Jack cheese chunks and roasted cashew pieces, with an oil-vinegar plus honey dressing. Tomato wedges and sprouts could also be added.

Invisible Cheese

Use green cabbage and grated white cheese—Jack, Provolone, or Fontinella—seasoned with some finely cut onion. Dress with orange juice sweetened with honey or an oil-vinegar dressing.

With Nuts

Green cabbage with red peppers and roasted peanuts or red cabbage with grapes and walnuts.

With Fruit

Cabbage with sliced cucumber, cantaloupe, grapes, apple, peach, apricot, raisins, any of these are good. A sour cream or yogurt dressing is often used, and a bleu cheese dressing is also good here.

—Red cabbage with orange slices and lightly salted turnip slices, or grated turnip.

—Red cabbage with an avocado dressing in the center.

Chinese Cabbage

Makes a wonderful salad ingredient:

With tomato, avocado, Jack cheese, cucumber, sprouts, and hard-boiled egg which has been marinated in beet juice, then sliced.

—With sliced oranges and green onion.

With thinly sliced radishes (could be daikon) and cucumber (could be lemon cucumber) and chopped parsley; a dressing of oil, lemon juice and salt.

—With dressing of dark sesame oil and soy sauce with orange rind and toasted sesame seeds: six parts soy sauce to one part dark sesame oil.

Tangerine Cabbage with Onion French Dressing

green cabbage, red cabbage, tangerines
oil and vinegar dressing with minced onion, dry mustard, fresh
(or powdered) garlic, salt, pepper, sugar

Shred both red and green cabbage, peel and section tangerines, or use canned Mandarin oranges. Make an oil and vinegar dressing (p. 170), seasoned as above. Mix together cabbage and tangerine, dress lightly.

Kim Chee

This is a Korean pickle which the Japanese also make. It can be quite strong if you like hot stuff, or made more mild for salad eating.

head of cabbage, salt, garlic, fresh ginger, sesame seeds, red pepper

Cut the cabbage into quarters lengthwise, then into bite-size chunks. Place in a bowl or crock and mix in about 1½ tablespoons of salt. Press overnight (p. 12). Next day pour off the accumulated water and save it for soup. Take the cabbage and rinse it off if overly salty. Season with garlic, then with freshly grated ginger. Add some toasted sesame seeds and, at the end, some red pepper to taste. The red pepper is potent, and its strength comes in the after-taste, so easy does it. Taste the pickle as you add each seasoning so you know what is happening to it—you can make it as strong as you like. After seasoning, the pickle can be stored in glass jars in the refrigerator. The flavor improves with age.

For immediate use, slice the cabbage thinly, salt to taste and then add the remaining ingredients.

Summer Salads

With the exception of eggplant, all of the summer "fruit" vegetables make excellent raw salads.

Summer Salad Platter

green peppers, cucumber, tomato, avocado, summer squashes

Cut in slices, wedges, sections, strips—a variety of shapes. These vegetables can be delicious with just salt and pepper, or toss them separately with dressing, then arrange on serving platter.

Summer Salad with Summer Squash

*summer squashes (zucchini, crookneck, or scallop), cheese
chunks, onion, green pepper, salt, tabasco*

Again, play around and find out which cut makes the most pleasing
shapes. Perhaps the squash and tomatoes in larger pieces and the
onion and pepper minced. Or everything cut in small pieces with
the cheese grated? Season with salt and Tabasco, or a dash of
vinegar. Keep the taste of the fresh vegetables. For more hots add
garlic, watercress or nasturtium leaves; for cools add parsley or
mint.

Zucchini Salad

*zucchini (raw or lightly cooked), grated carrot, walnuts;
lemon juice, olive oil, salt, pepper, lemon peel, basil or
mint*

Cut the zucchini in thin strips or ovals. Add the grated carrot.
Dress with olive oil-lemon juice dressing seasoned with salt, pepper,
lemon peel, and basil or mint. Garnish with walnut pieces.

Eggplant Salad

*1-2 eggplants, tomatoes, mushrooms, olives, lemon;
¼ minced onion, 3 cloves garlic, 4 T lemon juice, 1 t salt,
¼ t pepper, 1 T sugar (honey)*

Cube and fry the eggplant (or use already cooked leftover eggplant, which will usually make an even more flavorful salad).
Mash and season with minced onion, garlic, lemon juice, salt,
papper and sugar. Add the tomatoes, mushrooms, olives. Garnish with lemon wedges.

Vegetable & Bean Salads

Mixed Vegetable Salad

This can be a hot or cold salad. No single ingredient is stressed.

Take your pick: onion, celery, turnip, carrot, green pepper, cauliflower, broccoli
oil, vinegar, salt or soy sauce, dark sesame oil

Cut the vegetables in thin strips, so that they can cook quickly. Three or more vegetables can be used. Heat oil and stir-fry vegetables for three minutes. Sprinkle on vinegar and salt, or soy sauce, cover, and steam for three minutes. Adjust seasoning and serve or transfer the vegetables to a bowl and let cool. Sprinkle with dark sesame oil when serving.

Beet Salads

cooked beets, red radishes, cucumber; olive oil, lemon juice, salt, pepper, celery seed, thyme, dill weed

Slice or chunk the salad ingredients. Mix up the dressing, tasting it with slices of vegetable. When this salad is first combined, the radish and cucumber will still have their own coloring. Later everything will be beet colored but the vegetables will have soaked up more of the flavors of the dressing.

Wilted Spinach Salads

These are fast and delicious. Tear or cut the spinach into bite size pieces.

spinach, 8 oz. tomato sauce, 2 T minced dry onion, 1/3 cup olive oil, grated cheese

Cook onions in the tomato sauce until they are plump, about four minutes over a low flame. Add the olive oil and heat for a couple of minutes. Pour onto the spinach and toss. Garnish with grated cheese.

Variations:
—Toss the spinach with a tahini or nut sauce (see Sauces).
—Garnish with toasted nuts.

Cooked Vegetable or Bean Salad — Marinated

raw or cooked vegetables: cauliflower, broccoli, peas, green
beans, asparagus; and/or cooked beans: garbanzos, lentils,
kidneys
fresh raw vegetables: onion, celery, green pepper, carrot,
parsley, tomato, radish
oil-vinegar dressing, well seasoned

Mix ingredients together, and marinate in dressing, half hour to
overnight. The vegetables and beans will absorb the dressing more
thoroughly if they are hot when the dressing is applied. Other
thinly cut raw vegetables or leftovers can be added at the same
time or later.

Garbanzo Bean Salad

(Serves 8)

2 cups cooked garbanzo beans, 2 stalks celery, 1 green pepper,
1 dill pickle, red radishes, tomatoes, 1 carrot, green onion,
parsley
½ cup olive oil, 1/3 cup wine vinegar or lemon juice

Mix up the dressing and combine it with the hot beans, or heat it
with the beans for deeper penetration. Some of the beans could be
mashed and mixed with the dressing. Cool. Cut the tomatoes in
wedges and the other vegetables into thin, shapely pieces, or chop,
grate or mince them. Add the rest of the ingredients to the beans
at any time, reserving the tomato wedges and some of the others
for garnishing.

Variations:
   —Other ingredients to consider using: mushrooms, green or
black olives, cheese, nuts.
   —Make any of the substitutions in the Cooked Vegetable or Bean
Salad recipe, or in the Outline for Making Salads.
   —Make any of the substitutions or additions suggested in the
Basic Oil and Vinegar (French) Dressing recipe.

For seasoning the dressing (which can also be heated):
   —Bay leaf, thyme, oregano, parsley, dry mustard, salt, pepper.
   —Garlic, basil, tarragon, chili powder, sugar, Tabasco, salt, pepper.
   —Garlic, salt, celery salt or celery seed, pepper, oregano, parsley.

Grain Salads

These could be considered a variation of the marinated salad. They can be made with freshly cooked or leftover grain. Here are some specific examples:

Curried Rice Salad – I.

rice, grapes, Mandarin oranges, raisins, celery, pineapple, curry powder
dressing: sour cream, concentrated orange juice and chutney

Curried Rice Salad – II.

rice, green peppers, pimiento, raisins, parsley, green onions
dressing: oil-vinegar dressing seasoned with curry powder
garnish with: tomato wedges, some of the greens

Two Other Rice Salads

I.

cooked rice, grated turnips, shredded cabbage, minced onion, grated carrot
dressing: oil, vinegar and soy sauce, salt (if necessary)

II.

rice, green peppers, tomato, olives, pimiento
dressing: olive oil, vinegar, salt, pepper, basil, oregano
garnish: thinly sliced green onion, grated cheese

Noodle Salad

Again, marinated salads. Here's one we've done:

cooked noodles, green onions, chunked cooked yams
cream cheese, olive oil, salt, oregano, dill weed

For the dressing, mix the oil gradually with the softened cream cheese until it is a suitable consistency. Season.

Tabbouli

This is a grain salad made with Bulgur wheat. The Bulgur wheat can be either cooked or simply soaked.

bulgur wheat, water, onion, green pepper, cucumber, tomato,
celery, red or green cabbage
olive oil, lemon juice, salt, pepper, mint, garlic

Soak the Bulgur wheat in twice as much water for two to four hours until it's tender. Drain any water that has not been absorbed and save it for soup or bread. Cut the vegetables finely (your choice of those listed)—thin strips, diced or minced. Mix the vegetables with the Bulgur wheat and apply the dressing. Adjust the seasoning.

Some other possibilities:
—Green onions, spinach, walnuts or almonds, olives, avocado, capers, sliced hard-boiled eggs.
—Season with basil if you don't have mint.

Salad Dressings

These are a matter of taste, but try to make something complementary to the salad and to the meal. Is there already a sauce or should the dressing be creamy? Is everything else spicy or should the dressing provide that? Maybe Parmesan cheese in the dressing instead of topping the sauce? If the salad is colorful, perhaps a clear dressing?

Making a large batch—double or more—of salad dressing is a great convenience, and also the flavors have a chance to develop. If the basic dressing you make is fairly simple, additional ingredients can be added for variation each time it is used.

Most of the dressings in this section are based on oil and vinegar. What else goes in? Take a look:

A Basic Recipe for
Oil & Vinegar (French) Dressing

oil: olive, safflower, corn
vinegar: white, cider, red wine vinegar, rice wine vinegar,
orange, lemon or lime juice
salt and pepper

Three parts oil to one part vinegar, or two parts oil to one part vinegar. Maybe even one part oil to one part vinegar. Start with any of these, season tentatively, and then taste-test it. Make sure it's stirred or shaken up, then dip in a piece of lettuce or vegetable. More oil, vinegar, salt or pepper can be easily added.

Other Seasoning:
garlic and dry mustard, powdered ginger

Season with pressed garlic, dry mustard and/or powdered ginger. My first cooking teacher used to say: "If it lacks body add salt. If it lacks bite add mustard. If it lacks flavor add garlic." One of the cooks at Tassajara says: "It's not right if I can taste or feel any one particular ingredient."

herbs, spices, dairy, other

From here on, the dressing can go in many directions. General and specific instructions follow.

Herb & Spice Dressing

Here is a partial list of some of the possible seasonings for herb or spice dressings. Add the herbs or spices in addition to, or in place of, the garlic and dry mustard.

sugar or honey
herbs: basil, thyme, parsley, marjoram, tarragon, oregano, rose-
mary, dill weed, sage, mint
spices: anise, curry, chili, cinnamon, allspice, cloves, mace,
coriander, paprika, dill seed

The sugar is not necessarily meant to be tasted, but to bring out the sweetness of the lettuce.

Try using the herbs and spices which complement the meal as well as the salad.

Foundation Dressing

This is an excellent dressing for most salads, to be used as is or built upon with the additions which follow.

2/3 cup oil, 1/3 cup lemon juice, 3/4 t salt, 1/4 t pepper, 1/2 t dry mustard, 3/8 t dry powdered ginger, 1-2 large cloves garlic

Combine the ingredients, shake or stir thoroughly, taste-test with a piece of lettuce.

Herb Dressing

Try using olive oil and red wine vinegar. Add basil, tarragon, and marjoram or thyme, along with a generous amount of chopped parsley.

Spicy or Piquant Dressing

Try seasoning with Tabasco, coriander, cumin seed, chili powder, or Worcestershire sauce.

Mild Dressing

Make the dressing with lime juice (omit the garlic and mustard) seasoned with parsley, mint, and chopped green onion. Add a small amount of honey for flavor.

Sherman Dressing

Season the Foundation Dressing with curry powder and anise seed.

Cheese Dressing

Start with a basic oil and vinegar dressing (the Foundation recipe is fine) and add cream cheese and dill weed. Mix in a blender or soften the cream cheese by adding dressing to it a little at a time. Add bleu cheese in small pieces.

Fruit Salad Dressing

Use the Foundation recipe and omit the garlic and dry mustard, but leave in the powdered ginger. Add 1/3 cup of honey, along with a tablespoon or more of poppy seeds. One teaspoon of onion juice, minced or dry onion can also be added.

Easy Oriental Dressing

For all its simplicity this dressing is nevertheless still quite tasty. Use it on a delicate salad, or to lighten the feeling of a meal which seems heavy.

6 T oil, 2 T rice wine vinegar, 4 t soy sauce

Combine thoroughly. Taste and adjust if necessary.

Variations:
—Use another vinegar, or use lemon juice, in place of the rice wine vinegar.
—Add a few drops of dark sesame oil.
—Make it zingy with the addition of garlic, dry mustard or powdered ginger.

Creamy Dressings

These utilize the basic recipe for oil and vinegar dressing with the addition of a dairy product, mayonnaise, avocado, or honey.

Additions for a creamier dressing:

cream cheese (or neufchatel), sour cream, bleu cheese, grated cheese (parmesan is super), mayonnaise, avocado, egg, honey or sugar, grated onion, watercress, poppy seeds

These can be added for both flavor and texture. Use a creamy dressing to add "weight" to a salad or meal which is feeling too "light."

Mayonnaise Dressings

Mayonnaise already has the oil and vinegar mixed in—they've been beaten into egg yolks. These dressings have a pleasing, creamy quality, and give salads a medium weight. Though good with lettuce, they are especially suited to potato and other vegetable salads. Start with mayonnaise and season it thusly:

Soy Sauce Mayonnaise

Season mayonnaise with soy sauce. Curry, ginger, or garlic could be added for spiciness.

Bleu Cheese Mayonnaise

Season mayonnaise with bleu cheese, dry mustard, salt, pepper.

Russian Dressing

Season mayonnaise with chili sauce, minced peppers and onion, vinegar, paprika, salt and pepper.

Green Mayonnaise

Season with chopped green peppers, green onions, vinegar or lemon juice, tarragon, parsley or watercress, salt and pepper. Or season with avocado, green onion, lemon juice, garlic, salt and pepper.

Miscellaneous Dressings

Here are some other dressings which may suit what you have in the cupboard and refrigerator:

Yogurt Dressing

½ cup yogurt, 1 T orange juice, 2 T olive oil, ½ t tarragon, salt, pepper

Mix ingredients thoroughly and season to taste.

Avocado Dressings

1 avocado, 2/3 cup buttermilk, salt, pepper, garlic

Mash the avocado with the buttermilk and season to taste.

Or:

> *1 avocado, ½ cup sour cream, 2 T lemon juice, salt, pepper, minced onion*

Mash the avocado with the sour cream and lemon juice, and season.

Peanut Butter Salad Dressing

> *6 T peanut butter, ½ cup water, ¼ cup finely chopped green onion, 1 t vinegar, ½ t dry mustard, ¼ t thyme, salt, garlic salt*

Mix and adjust seasoning to taste.

Tahini Salad Dressing

> *½ cup tahini, ¼ cup lemon juice, ½ cup water, soy sauce*

Mix and adjust seasoning to taste.

Soups

Soups can have either a thick or thin base (background). *Thicker soups* can be based on beans, potatoes, winter squashes, grains, nut butters, or a flour-thickened sauce. For *thinner soups* the background is generally water or vegetable stock with added seasonings.

Thin Soups

The basic idea is quite simple: vegetables in liquid. What varies are the vegetables used and how long they are cooked. Cabbage may be simmered five minutes and still be somewhat chewy, or simmered half an hour and flavor the stock more thoroughly. Having few vegetables may make the soup sparse or elegant. Many vegetables can make the soup a main course, or overly heavy.

Outline for Thin Soups

(Serves 4-6)

4 cups water, stock, or tomato juice

Heat the stock. Start with less liquid if you are planning a soup with many vegetables.

sliced, chunked, or diced vegetables: just a few, or up to 2½ cups, or more (also cooked grains or beans in place of vegetables)
noodles: add with the vegetables 25-30 minutes before serving

Since they will be prominent, give some careful attention to cutting the vegetables. Add them to the stock and simmer—don't boil! —until tender.

Or (for a different flavor and faster cooking): Sauté the vegetables first, then add them to the stock and simmer.

seasonings: salt, pepper
salty—soy sauce, miso; hot—garlic, grated ginger; tang—lemon juice or peel, orange juice or peel; herb—thyme, marjoram, basil, mint
flavor: sweet—sugar, honey; sour—vinegar, lemon juice

Season lightly, starting with salt at the beginning, and adjust the seasoning at the end.

enrichments: eggs and cheese

Eggs or cheese may be added.

garnishings: aside from the standard ones, radish slices, sprouts, other finely cut greens, or thinly sliced lemon or orange

Garnish the soup if you wish.

Making Stock

Using a vegetable stock instead of water will give any soup a more full-bodied flavor. Vegetable stocks can come from water saved after cooking vegetables, or be made from scraps or fresh vegetables.

Vegetable Stock

vegetable scraps: almost anything—ends, tips, tops, trimmings, roots, skins, parsley stems, outside cabbage leaves, limp vegetables. Go easy on the green pepper centers. Some people find a large amount of onion skins or carrot tops makes too strong a flavor.
water to cover

Place all the vegetable scraps, which may be chopped up first, in a saucepan or stockpot and cover with water. It's important that this brew simmer rather than boil. Simmering means a few wee bubbles are popping gently to the surface—a quiet, subdued leaching process, while boiling means that the entire surface is in turmoil,

176

bubbling and frothing. Vegetables do not endure boiling very well, soon yielding their more rank flavors and aromas, so bring the stock to a simmer and then turn the heat down low enough to keep it there, or you will have a harsh-flavored stock.

Let the stock simmer an hour or more, and then strain out the vegetables, squeezing or mashing out the last juices. Use in place of water for soups, or for cooking vegetables, grains or beans. If not using immediately, leave uncovered until cool, then cover and refrigerate.

To make the most of your vegetable trimmings, make this stock every day. Start it while you are preparing the meal, adding all the trimmings as you go. Use a little water from the stock to rinse out each pot. Simmer through the meal and then strain it afterwards. This kind of stock will keep indefinitely if it is simmered (with new additions) at least once a week. To give it a lift add a few onion, garlic or ginger slices.

Mock Beef Stock

This makes an excellent stock and, depending on how you cut the vegetables, quite a beautiful one.

onion, carrot, celery
grated fresh ginger or garlic, sprig of chinese parsley, soy sauce

Don't worry if you don't have the ginger and Chinese parsley. The vegetables give a fine flavor also. Dice the onions, cut the carrot in thin half moons, and cut the celery in thin pieces. Season the water or stock, heat to boiling, and add the vegetables. Simmer for ten minutes. Add soy sauce and salt to taste.

Soy sauce broths make an especially good base for egg flower soups (p. 180). Peas and green onions complement egg flower soup nicely.

Adding Vegetables to the Soup

There are basically two ways of adding vegetables to a soup base: sautéing them first, and putting them into the soup raw. (Leftover cooked vegetables can also be added to soup.) Either way, be sure that they are cut to spoon-size or smaller. The flavor of both the soup base and the vegetables will vary, depending on whether or not the vegetables were precooked.

177

Sautéed:

If the vegetables are to be cooked only briefly in the soup, they will need a more lengthy sautéing first, and if they are to be cooked at greater length in the soup, they will require less sautéing.

When frying the vegetables, start with the onion, as it seems to draw out and unite the flavors of the other vegetables. After sautéing the vegetables for several minutes, a few spoonfuls of flour can be added. The flour helps to thicken the soup and to suspend the vegetables. Stir it in and cook it with the vegetables for five minutes, and then add everything to the soup base. Put some liquid back into the frying pan and heat gently to incorporate stray juices, flour and oil. Add this to the soup.

Raw:

Vegetables such as mushrooms, spinach, chard, peas, which require little cooking, can be kept out of the sauté and added to the soup raw, three to five minutes before serving. The same is true of finely cut or grated vegetables such as green pepper or carrot.

When adding raw vegetables to the soup base, figure out how long each thing needs to cook. This depends not only on what it is, but also on the size of the pieces. Here's a basic rundown for simmered vegetables. (For faster cooking, cut into smaller pieces.)

potatoes, beets, onions	50 minutes
carrots, broccoli, cauliflower	30 minutes
celery, green beans, asparagus	20 minutes
corn, zucchini	10 minutes
peas, tomatoes, cabbage, chard, spinach, green onion, parsley	5 minutes or less

With some attention to timing, vegetables can retain much of their original taste, color and texture, as well as flavoring the soup. For vegetable mush, there's nothing to it: just put all the vegetables in the pot at once and simmer for an hour.

Some vegetables, though, such as tomatoes or cabbage, can go in early or late with a variety of effects.

Keep in mind that potato can be the chunky foreground as well as the mushed background, and that cauliflower can be the backdrop as well as the floating flowerette . . . whatever suits the ingredients and the occasion.

Seasoning Soups

Spare yourself an overpowering dose of herbs, vinegar, sugar, pepper. What is usually missing from any soup is . . . salt! Add this first to see what flavors are already present. If it's on the sweet side, the remedy is to make it sweet-and-peppery or sweet-and-sour: pepper, garlic, ginger or a bit of lemon juice. To pick up a vegetable broth add thyme, marjoram, or mint and cloves. Other medleys (remedies) are mentioned where they come up.

Using Soy Sauce and Miso:
We use them often at Tassajara for seasoning both thin and thick soups. Here's how:

Adding soy sauce: This is a matter of taste. With a gentle hand the soy sauce does not overpower the flavor of the vegetables, but brings it out. Add a little salt along with the soy sauce, so that the soy flavor does not get too strong.

Adding miso: Miso is a fermented soybean paste, which is easily digestible and which adds protein and other nourishment as well as flavor. Like soy sauce, miso is salty, but if it is relied on to supply all of the soup's saltiness, its flavor will be quite strong. For four cups of soup broth, start with about three tablespoons of miso. Mix it with a small amount of hot soup to thin it out, then add it to the rest of the soup just before serving. An alternative way is to put the miso in a strainer and, dipping the strainer into the soup, stir the miso with the soup liquid and sieve it into the soup. Once the miso is added, taste the soup and see whether you want a stronger miso flavor or just more salt.

Adding Enrichments

Grated Cheese: Swiss, cheddar, Parmesan, Edam, Jack, and other cheeses can be grated and added to any soup, either garnishing the surface of the soup or disappearing into it. Make the addition just before serving.

Adding cream: Gently heated cream can be added to the soup just before serving. After adding the cream to the soup, heat it but don't boil. Check the seasoning.

Adding egg yolks and cream: This is a classic enrichment. Of course it's delicious, but isn't the soup already tasty? Beat the yolks with the cream, and beat some hot soup gradually into them. Mix everything back into the soup and heat gently, being careful not to boil.

Egg in Your Soup:

There are basically two ways to add raw eggs to soup. One is the "egg-drop" or "egg flower" method, and the other is a thorough blending. One other possibility is to poach eggs in the soup.

For *Egg Flower Soup,* a light, clearish broth with or without vegetables is probably best. Just before serving, bring the broth to a gently rolling boil, and pour in the barely beaten eggs. Stir slightly and watch the eggs puff up and float around in various flowery shapes.

For concealed egg enrichment, beat the eggs and then, just before serving, beat in some of the hot soup a little at a time. When the eggs are thoroughly heated, beat the whole mixture back into the rest of the soup. Further cooking at this time will cause the eggs to scramble (or particle-ize). If you don't want this, don't cook after adding the eggs.

—Beat soy sauce or lemon juice into the eggs before adding the hot soup.

—For a more foamy soup, separate the eggs and beat the whites until stiff. Beat a cup of hot soup into the egg yolks (with soy or lemon?) and return this mixture to the main body of the soup. Then fold in the whites.

Thin soups included are: Cabbage Family Soups, Beet Soups, Lettuce or Greens Soups, Onion Soup, Tomato Soup, Miso and Soy Sauce Soups.

Cabbage Family Soups

Where the recipe calls for cabbage, broccoli, cauliflower or Brussels sprouts can all be used. Remember—for succulent, rather than noxious, flavors, these vegetables should be simmered rather than boiled, and that their flavor changes the more they are cooked.

Simple Cabbage Soup

4 cups water or stock, an onion, half head of cabbage, a carrot, mustard greens, salt, pepper, celery seed, caraway seed, poppy seed

Except for the mustard greens, cut the vegetables in spoon size pieces. It is usually best to cut a single vegetable all in the same shape. Add the vegetables and a moderate amount of the seasonings to the stock and simmer for about thirty minutes. Adjust the seasoning and add the finely cut mustard greens shortly before serving.

Variations:
   —Make any of the substitutions in the Outline for Thin Soups.
   —For *Five Vegetable Cabbage Soup*, add celery and potato. Season with garlic and marjoram, basil or thyme.
   —Serve purple! For *Red Cabbage Soup*, use red cabbage in place of green. One simple combination is with onion, using sliced red radishes for garnish. For crisper cabbage, add it in the last five to ten minutes.
   —For *Main Course Cabbage Soup*, get out the leftovers. This may turn into a stew. In addition to the onion, carrot and cabbage, use potatoes, turnip, leftover beans or grain. Season with garlic, thyme, half bay leaf, powdered clove (pinch), parsley and Chinese parsley (celantro). Add the onion, carrots and potatoes first. With about twenty minutes to go, add the cabbage (broccoli, cauliflower, green beans). Adjust the seasoning. Pass around bowls of sliced hard-boiled eggs, grated cheese, sour cream, sliced green onion for garnishing.
   —For *Cabbage Borscht*, season any of the preceding cabbage soups in the last five minutes with juice of one or two lemons, ¼ cup of sugar or honey. Serve with side bowls of sour cream or yogurt. Vinegar can replace the lemon juice.

Beet Soups

A very small amount of beets turns "Cabbage Soup" into "Beet Soup." Add the beets in addition to, or in place of, the cabbage. Already cooked beets can go in early or late. Otherwise, start cooking the chunked or sectioned beets fifty to sixty minutes before serving. Some of the raw or cooked beets could be grated. Use any of the vegetable or seasoning combinations listed under cabbage soups, including the preceding Cabbage Borscht.

Simple Beet Soup

4 cups water, 1 onion, 3-4 beets, beet greens, salt, pepper,
lemon juice, sugar or honey

Scrub the beets and, leaving the skins on, grate them or cut them
into small pieces. Dice and sauté the onions and cook them with
the beets in the water until they are tender, about thirty to forty-
five minutes. Season moderately with salt, pepper, lemon and
sugar. Add the sectioned beet greens. Cook for a couple of minutes
more.

Chard Soup

4 cups water or stock, 2 onions (sliced), bunch of chard (one
pound), salt, pepper, garlic, parsley, 2 eggs, beaten (sour
cream, yogurt)

Cut the chard once lengthwise, then crosswise in half-inch sections.
Cut the stalks in quarter-inch slices. Sauté the onion until it is transparent, and add it to the stock along with the chard. Season with
salt, pepper, garlic and parsley. Simmer ten to thirty minutes. Beat
some of the hot soup into the eggs, then beat this mixture back
into the soup. Serve immediately, accompanied by some sour
cream or yogurt if handy.

Variations:
   —Make any of the substitutions suggested in the Outline for Thin
Soups.
   —This soup can be done with spinach, mustard greens, Brussels
sprouts, cabbage, lettuce and other vegetables.
   —Try seasoning moderately with soy sauce or lemon juice. These
can be added to the soup or beaten in with the eggs before they are
added.

Onion Soup

This is such a simple soup, but for onion lovers it's fantastic. The
onions get quite sweet.

4 cups water or stock, 4-6 onions (2½-3 cups), 4T flour, salt,
pepper, soy sauce, oil

Slice the onions thinly and sauté them until they begin to brown—about fifteen to twenty minutes. Use butter or oil for the frying. Olive oil or corn germ oil gives added flavor. Sprinkle flour over the onions, mix it in, cover and steam for five to ten minutes, opening to stir once or twice. (The flour will give added body as in the thickened soup recipes.) Add to the heated water or stock. Scrape out the frying pan with some of the soup liquid and return it to the soup. Season with the salt and soy sauce, along with the pepper. Simmer for at least half an hour to develop the flavor. Onions can be cooked and cooked. Correct the seasoning and serve.

Some people feel this soup should be served the second day after it is made. Then it's "even better."

Variations:
—Add butter or cream before serving.
—Add a little wine or brandy.
—Add croutons, which have been sautéed in olive oil and garlic.
—Add Parmesan cheese as a garnish.

Tomato Soups

Tomatoes are like beets. Adding them to a vegetable soup soon makes it tomato soup with vegetables. Tomato sauce, tomato paste, cooked and sieved tomatoes, or fresh tomato sections can all be used to make Cabbage Soup into Tomato-Cabbage Soup, Spinach Soup into Tomato-Spinach Soup. (If you don't plan to sieve or purée fresh tomatoes, cut them into small pieces to start with.) Using tomato juice for the stock does it too. Here are some other simple tomato soup recipes:

Onion-Tomato Soup

4 cups water or stock, onion, tomatoes, salt, pepper, oregano or marjoram, parsley, finely cut greens, grated parmesan cheese

Sauté onions. Add sliced tomatoes and cook for five minutes. Season and then simmer for fifteen minutes. Sieve for smooth soup. Add the water or stock. Heat. Check seasoning. Serve with grated Parmesan cheese.

Variations:
—Make any of the substitutions in the Outline for Thin Soups.
—Add heated milk (with cream) instead of water or stock.
—Season with sugar, basil, salt, pepper and brandy.
—Sauté celery or carrot or green pepper with the onion, before adding the tomato.
—May also be seasoned with thyme, sage or basil.
—Tomato lends itself to peppery seasonings: Tabasco sauce, cayenne pepper, horseradish, Worcestershire sauce.

Thick Soups

Bean Soups

If you have some question about cooking beans, see the Bean section. These soups are particularly satisfying in colder weather when fewer fresh ingredients are available.

A Basic Recipe for Bean Soups
(For 4-6)

1 cup beans: lentils, split peas, navy beans, limas, pintos, etc.
5-6 cups water or unsalted stock

Rinse off the beans. Soak, and cook them until tender—by simmering or pressure cooking. If you wish to, drain the beans and mash or purée them.

diced or sliced vegetables: onions, green peppers, celery, carrot, potatoes, tomatoes, mushrooms, others (can be leftovers); greens: sliced finely

Sauté the diced vegetables for three to five minutes and add them to the beans for ten to fifteen minutes or longer.
Add sliced greens for the last three to five minutes.

seasonings: salt, pepper, herbs, garlic

Season tentatively when the beans are tender, then again a few minutes before serving. (Once they are thick, bean soups burn easily, so as a rule keep the heat low.)

garnishings: parsley, green onions, grated cheese, alfalfa sprouts, etc.

Garnish the soup for added flavor, nutrition or invitation.

Options:
—Onions are especially suited for cooking along with beans for added flavor.

—Potatoes may need more cooking than suggested above. Add them to the beans sooner than the other vegetables.

—Soy sauce can be used in place of some of the salt.

For another approach to bean soups, take any of the bean dishes in the Beans section and make it thinner.

Here are some specific variations:

Lentil Soup

1 cup lentils, 5-6 cups water, an onion, a stalk or two of celery, a carrot, salt, pepper, ½-1 bay leaf, 1-2 cloves garlic, thyme, rosemary

Wash the lentils, add the water and garlic, and pressure cook them for fifteen minutes, or simmer them for an hour and a half. Meanwhile slice or dice the vegetables and sauté them for five minutes. When the beans are tender, add the sautéed vegetables and season with the salt, pepper and herbs. Put the whole cloves and bay leaf in a cheesecloth bag or metal tea caddy if you wish to retrieve them before serving the soup. Simmer for fifteen minutes. Check the seasoning and serve.

Here are some other lentil soups:
—*Lentil Soup with Lentil Sprouts:* Use a cup or so of lentil sprouts in place of, or in addition to, the celery or carrots. Add the sprouts a few minutes before serving.

—*Mint Lentil Soup:* Use salt, mint and marjoram for the seasoning.

—*With Lemon:* Cut a lemon (unpeeled) in quarters lengthwise, then slice thinly crosswise. Add the lemon to the lentils along with the sautéed vegetables. Lighten or omit other seasonings.

—*With Potatoes:* Lentils make an excellent gravy for potatoes or they can go in soup together. Cube the potatoes and cook them in a cup or two of the water, while the beans are cooking, then combine. Leftover potatoes, chunked or mashed, can be added. Leftover potato salad doesn't make much of a potato soup, but it's okay in lentil soup. Seasoning can be the same or varied.

—Split Pea Soup: Use split peas in place of lentils. They cook into a creamy soup base without mashing, puréing or blending. Split pea soup is good plain, with the lentil soup seasoning, or any of the following: (in addition to salt and pepper) basil or marjoram, caraway seeds, fennel and anise seeds, miso.

—With Greens: Split pea and lentil soups can absorb a lot (of vegetables, abuse, seasonings). Greens go well here. Slice them finely and add three to five minutes before serving.

Navy Bean Soup

1 cup navy beans, 2-3 onions, 2-3 stalks celery, salt, sage, oregano, celery seed, soy sauce

This recipe is intended to emphasize the real goodness of bean flavor, so stay away from garlic and tomatoes as these have a tendency to overpower the beans. Cook the beans with the onion until they are tender. Sauté the celery for five minutes and add it. Season, being careful to let the bean and onion flavor predominate. Taste it! Basil is good too, or a little rosemary. Can be garnished with parsley or green onions.

Make any of the substitutions listed in the basic recipe for bean soups. Here are a few in particular:

—Lima Bean Soup: Use lima beans in place of the navy beans. Use mushrooms and peas for the vegetables. When the beans are cooked, some of them could be mashed or blended. Add the peas and sliced mushrooms five minutes before serving. Check the seasoning.

—Mixed Bean Soup: Use a combination of beans totaling one cup—say split peas, red kidneys and small limas.

—Garbanzo Bean Soup: Use garbanzo beans in place of the navy beans, and (getting farther from the recipe) season with: lemon juice, garlic, soy sauce, tahini (if you have it). Garnish with plenty of parsley.

An Unofficial Recipe for Minestrone

Bean soups are famous for their ability to consume leftovers. They can take vegetables, grains, potatoes, pasta, eggs, cheese, stale bread, even salads. When the leftover bean soup comes out well, somebody makes up a recipe as though it were made with fresh ingredients. Such is Minestrone. No wonder people disagree as to what goes into it. The way it's made is to clean out your refrigerator and your bread box, cut everything into spoon-size pieces, and add it to a bean soup with tomato, onion, garlic, oregano, thyme, basil, with Parmesan cheese sprinkled on top. Do people really cook up a third of a cup of macaroni just to put into Minestrone soup? Or put out bread a week ahead to get it stale in time? I hope not.

Variations:
   —Be selective.
      Try it again next week.

Bean Stew: If the bean soup is real thick with lots of vegetables, call it a "stew." Simmer it over low heat or put it in the oven to bake.

Grain Soups

These are very similar to bean soups in their make-up, with grain replacing beans. Although grains won't mash the way beans will, the longer they are cooked the softer they get and the thicker they make the soup.

Basic Grain Soup Recipe

*¾ cup dry grain: especially rice, barley or buckwheat;
any other whole or cracked grain: bulgur wheat, cracked
wheat, corn meal, oatmeal, etc.
5-6 cups water or stock*

Cook the washed grain in the water or stock at a gentle boil for an hour or longer.

sliced or diced vegetables: onion, celery, carrot, tomatoes, other

Add the vegetables about half an hour before the end of cooking. Or sauté the vegetables first for five minutes and add to the grain for the last ten to fifteen minutes of cooking.

*seasonings: salt, pepper; herbs: often thyme, sage, rosemary and
parsley; garlic and soy sauce*

Season to taste.

garnishings: grated cheese, parsley, green onions, so forth

Garnish.

This soup is an obvious place to use leftover grains. Substitute 1½-2 cups of cooked grain for the raw grain. Use somewhat less water unless you find it is all needed.

Grains can also be used to thicken other soups. Whole grains like barley, brown rice and wheat berries will add a certain amount of chewiness, as well as thickening. Replace a quarter cup of beans with a quarter cup of grain, or add it in addition to the beans, and cook as usual.

For *Nut Buttered Grain Soup* add ¼-½ cup of nut butter towards the end of cooking. Thin it first with some of the hot soup, then stir it in.

Here are some specific recipes and variations:

Cheese, Rice & Tomato Soup

¾ cup rice, 5 cups water, an onion, 4-5 tomatoes, salt, pepper, ¼ lb. grated cheese

Start the rice cooking in the water, then slice or dice the onion, and cut the tomatoes in small pieces. Sauté the onion for five to ten minutes, then add the tomatoes for several minutes. After the rice has cooked for thirty minutes, add the onion and tomato and continue simmering. Season with the salt and pepper. Just before serving, stir in half of the grated cheese and use the remainder for a garnish.

Variations:

—Make any of the substitutions listed in the Basic Grain Soup Recipe.

—For *Cream of Tomato Rice Soup:* Cook the rice in 3 cups of water. Add 2 cups of gently heated milk along with the onion and tomato. Season with sugar and basil, along with salt and pepper. For a smoother soup, sieve or blend the onions and tomatoes before adding them to the cooking rice.

—For *Easy Tomato Rice Soup:* Cook the rice in 3 cups of water and, when it is tender, add 1-3 cups of heated tomato juice. Add bread cubes which have been fried in butter with garlic and oregano.

—For *Corn Meal Tomato Soup:* Use corn meal in place of the rice. (It will cook faster.) Cut the tomatoes in fat wedges and add them along with diced green pepper about six to eight minutes before serving, so that they retain their brightest color. Season with salt, pepper, thyme and chili powder. Garnish with minced parsley or sliced green onions, as well as cheese.

For *Barley Soup:* Use barley in place of rice and cook it for 1½ hours. Add sautéed carrot and turnip along with the onion and tomato.

Potato or Squash Soups

Some winter squash soups are also in the Winter Squash section.

Basic Potato Soup Recipe
(Serves 4-6)

> *4 medium potatoes, or sweet potatoes or yams, 2 lb. winter squash*
> *water to cover*

Scrub the potatoes and cut them into quarters or smaller. Cover with water, bring to boil, then simmer until the potatoes are tender. Strain off, reserve the cooking liquid, and mash the potatoes.

> *a cup or more sliced, chunked, or diced vegetables: onions, leeks, celery, carrot, green beans, peas, greens*
> *a cup or more milk, water (cream, sour cream, buttermilk)*

Sauté the vegetables starting with the onion, and add them to the mashed potatoes along with the reserved cooking liquid and enough milk or stock to bring the soup to desired thickness.

> *seasonings: salt, pepper, chervil, marjoram, basil, garlic*

Season with salt, pepper and herbs.

> *enrichments and garnishings: grated cheese, eggs, cream, green onion, chives, parsley, watercress*

Sprinkle with paprika and sliced green onions when serving.

Vegetables such as peas, mushrooms, spinach or chard which require little cooking do not need to be sautéed. Add them to the soup four or five minutes before serving.

This soup is an obvious place to use leftover potatoes—mashed, boiled, or baked. Chop up boiled or baked potatoes before adding them.

Potato-Watercress Soup

4 medium potatoes, an onion, 2 bunches watercress, 2 T flour, 2 cups water, 3 cups milk, salt, pepper

Cube the potatoes and start them cooking in the water. Dice the onion and mince the watercress, cutting the stems finely crosswise. Sauté the onions for several minutes, then add the watercress and continue cooking. Start the milk heating gently. Add the flour to the vegetables and cook for three minutes, before gradually stirring in the heated milk. When the potatoes are tender, drain them and reserve the liquid. Mash the potatoes and combine with the reserved liquid and the vegetable-milk sauce. Season with salt and pepper and simmer until serving.

For an entirely smooth soup, add just one cup of milk to the onions and watercress, then sieve or blend them, before combining with the remainder of the milk and the potatoes.

Variations:
—Use any of the substitutions suggested in the Basic Potato Soup Recipe, including sweet potatoes, yams or squash in place of potatoes and the vegies.
—*Adding cheese:* With or without the watercress, try adding grated cheese. Parmesan or another white cheese can be stirred in for a hidden enrichment. Cheddar cheese with sliced green onions or parsley makes a colorful garnish.

Cream Soups

When a soup has a thick and "creamy" consistency, it is known as "cream soup" even if it doesn't have any dairy cream. Cream soups are usually thickened with flour. Milk or cream may or may not be used.

Basic Recipe for Cream of Vegetable Soup
(Serves 4-6)

The plan is to cook the vegetables and add them to a flour-thickened sauce.

3 T oil: corn, soy, safflower, olive; butter or margarine
4 T flour: white, whole wheat, barley, rye, buckwheat, corn meal, etc.

To start the sauce, cook the flour in the oil for two to five minutes, or longer for darker color. Use different flours or oils to change the flavor.

3 cups heated milk, water, stock, tomato juice, etc.

Remove the pan from the heat and pour in the heated milk. Stir briskly and scrape the bottom and corners of the pan to incorporate all of the oil-flour mixture. Season and simmer.

a cup or more sliced, chunked or diced vegetables: onion, celery, carrot, green pepper, mushrooms, cauliflower, corn, asparagus, etc.
½ cup water

Sauté the vegetables, starting with the onion, for five minutes. Add the half cup of water, cover and steam until tender. If desired, sieve or blend the vegetables before combining them with the sauce.

seasonings: salt, pepper, nutmeg or mace, herbs

Simmer the vegetables with the sauce, while adjusting the seasoning.

enrichments and garnishings: grated cheese, eggs, cream, green onion, chives, parsley, watercress

Garnish and serve.

This is one of the soups into which old vegetables can disappear, especially if the vegetables are sieved before being added to the sauce. For more seasoning possibilities see Sauces.

Cream Soup with Vegetables

3 T oil, 4 T flour, 3 cups heated milk; an onion, 2 stalks celery,
2 carrots; ½ cup water; salt, pepper, celery seed

Slice the onion and celery and cut the carrots in matchstick pieces.
Make the sauce as directed in the Basic Recipe for Cream of Vegetable Soup, season it with the salt, pepper and celery seed, and let
it simmer while the vegetables are sauté-steamed. Combine the
vegetables and the sauce, adjust the seasoning, and use the minced
celery leaves for a garnish.

Variations:
　—Make any of the substitutions suggested in the Basic Recipe
for Cream of Vegetable Soup.
　—For *Spicy Cream of Vegetable Soup,* use onions and green
peppers and season with garlic and dry mustard.
　—For *Creamed Squash Soup,* use either summer or winter
squash. Sauté-steam it, then mash it and add it to the sauce.
Season with basil or oregano.
　—For *Cream of Mushroom Soup,* use a generous amount of
mushrooms (½-1 pound), along with some onion for flavor and
a little carrot or celery for color. Chopped olives can garnish this
soup. Brandy can flavor it.

Cream of Spinach (or Lettuce) Soup

This recipe is intended to demonstrate another way of preparing
a cream of vegetable soup. The flour is cooked with the sautéing
vegetables, then liquid is added to make the sauce.

2 bunches of spinach or 2 heads of lettuce (red leaf or butter),
an onion, clove of garlic, chopped parsley, salt, pepper,
4 T flour, 2 cups water (heated), 2 cups milk or more,
oil for sautéing

Slice the onion and spinach (or lettuce) in fine shreds. Sauté the
onion for several minutes in 3-4 tablespoons of oil or butter. Add
the spinach, salt, pepper, pressed garlic and chopped parsley and
continue cooking to wilt the greens. Add the flour and cook it for
several minutes, before removing the pan from the heat and stirring

in the heated water. Cover and simmer for ten minutes. Force
through a fine sieve, purée in a blender (or leave it as is), then add
the milk. Heat and correct seasonings. Serve garnished with parsley.

Variations:
    —Make any of the changes suggested in the Basic Recipe for
Cream of Vegetable Soup.
    —Use lettuce, chard, mustard greens, cabbage, Brussels sprouts
in place of the spinach.
    —Add one or two eggs for enrichment.
    —For *Cream of Carrot Soup,* use grated carrots in place of the
spinach. Use buckwheat flour if you like it. Season this soup with
a bit of thyme or sage. Wheat germ is good here too.
    —For *Cream of Tomato with Mushrooms,* use onion and mush-
rooms for the vegetables. In place of the milk, use tomato juice.
Season with basil or tarragon in addition to salt and pepper.
    —For *Cream of Onion with Cheese,* use 4-6 onions. Sauté for
fifteen minutes before adding the flour. Season with added garlic
and a pinch or two of powdered ginger. Add grated cheese just
before serving.

Cold Soups

Many of the preceding soups are suitable for serving cold, as well
as hot. What follows are three ways by which soups can be adapted
for serving cold—1) adding milk or cream, 2) adding salad dressing,
3) making sweet-sour.

Adding Milk or Cream

    (This also includes adding sour cream, yogurt, buttermilk.)
Perhaps these soups are good because we associate dairy products
with coldness. Start with a potato soup, split pea soup, a squash
soup, a sweet potato soup. If you know that you are making a cold
soup, make the base soup thicker than usual, so that it can stand
being diluted with milk or cream. You may or may not want pieces
of cooked vegetable floating in the smoothness of these soups.

    hot soup: potato, split pea, squash, sweet potato

Start with one of these soups, which can be leftover. If you are
making it from scratch, make it thicker than usual.

193

vegetables: same as for the hot soup

Vegetables, cooked as usual, can be puréed or left in small pieces.

dairy: milk, cream, yogurt, sour cream, buttermilk

Buttermilk or yogurt adds a flavorful tartness to these soups. Chill the soup, then add the milk.

seasonings: same as for the hot soup, or take your pick of garlic, dill, thyme, pepper, basil, dry mustard, lemon peel

Adjust the seasoning.

garnishings: green onion, parsley, cucumber, chopped hard-boiled egg

Garnish with sliced green onion, etc.

Raw vegetables: Diced or finely sliced raw vegetables can be added for chewing interest and fresh flavor. Onions, green peppers, cucumber are often used for this purpose.

Yogurt Soup

This cold soup can also be made starting with yogurt and milk, buttermilk and milk, yogurt and buttermilk, or even homemade yogurt which didn't thicken. Add raw, freshly diced or minced vegetables—onion, celery, peppers, cucumbers, parsley, summer squashes, watercress. Season with garlic, dill, possibly lemon juice, as well as salt and pepper. Chill and serve.

Cool Greens

onion; lettuce or sorrel (sour grass) or spinach or swiss chard; salt, garlic

This recipe is based on the Spinach Soup, page 192.

As in that recipe, sauté the onion and add it, along with the garlic and the finely cut greens, to 2 cups of water. Simmer for twenty minutes. Purée at this time, if you want a homogenous soup. Cool the soup. Add 2 cups or more sour cream, yogurt, buttermilk, milk or cream. Adjust seasoning: salt, pepper, garlic, plus thyme, dill.

Garnish with (or pass dishes of) chopped hard-boiled egg, sliced green onions, parsley, cucumber.

Adding Salad Dressing

These cold soups are basically liquid salads: a lot of finely minced or blended vegetables with salad dressing for flavoring, plus additional liquid. The most famous of these is *Gazpacho*. Here's the idea—for 4-6 servings.

Gazpacho

> *vegetables: onion, celery, green pepper, small cucumber,*
> *3-4 tomatoes, parsley*
> *liquid: 2 cups tomato juice*

The vegetables are used raw. Dice, mince or blend, and add them to the tomato juice.

> *dressing: 1/3 cup olive oil, 3 T red wine vinegar; garlic, salt,*
> *pepper, (tabasco,) basil, tarragon*

Mix up the dressing and combine thoroughly with the other ingredients. Adjust the seasonings, including the oil and vinegar. If you like garlic, use it freely in this recipe. Basil or tarragon goes well with tomatoes.

Variations to this recipe are easily come by:

—Use other vegetables which are edible raw—carrot, summer squashes, cabbage, etc.

—If you like grains or beans served this way, add a moderate amount of either, cooked. Among others, rice, Bulgur wheat, garbanzos, lentils are all adaptable to this recipe.

—Season the dressing some other way: Omit the garlic and season with mint. Use soy sauce in place of salt. See Salad Dressings for other ideas.

Sweet-Sour Cold Soups

This is a third way of making a cold soup appetizing. See the Cabbage and Beet Soups, which offer many ways to do this and many vegetable combinations to use. Cook up the soup. Season tentatively. Cool. Adjust the seasoning. Often, sour cream is served with these cold sweet and sour soups, and with tomato soups, greens soup, vegetables soups too.

Sauces

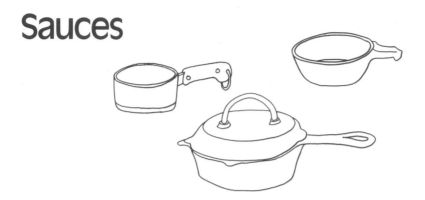

Sauces come about in a variety of ways, but usually they are based on some finely ground starch which thickens a liquid into a sauce. Other kinds of sauces are based on tomatoes, nuts, beans, cream cheese.

Sauces naturally complement the dry and the chewy, and have the capacity to be both soothing and exciting, reassuring and invigorating. To use a sauce is to take one more step—bringing a new panorama into view, or making food just more tiring. Care is needed. Use sauces to dress up stuffed vegetables or pastries, to accompany grain, pasta, bean or vegetable dishes, and to cover up mistakes and unwanted plainness.

Flour Sauces

White and Brown

The basis of a white sauce is butter-flour-*milk,* while the basis of a brown sauce is a butter-flour-*stock or water.* Every added ingredient changes the name of the sauce, if you're keeping track in French.

Thickness of the sauce: The ratio of flour to liquid determines the thickness of the sauce:

1 T flour to 1 cup liquid   — a thin sauce
1½ T flour to 1 cup liquid — a medium-thick sauce
2 T flour to 1 cup liquid   — a thick sauce
3 T flour to 1 cup liquid   — a very thick sauce
4 T flour to 1 cup liquid   — departs from the realm of sauces and enters the realm of puddings

196

Basic Recipe

For each cup of (medium-thick) sauce:

White Sauce:

> *2 T butter or oil: mild-flavored oil*
> *2 T flour: white, rice, barley, corn flour*
> *1 cup heated liquid: milk*
> *basic seasonings: salt, white pepper*

Brown Sauce:

> *2 T butter or oil: sesame, peanut, corn germ oil*
> *2 T flour: white, whole wheat, barley, buckwheat, rye,*
> *corn flour*
> *1 cup heated liquid: water or vegetable stock (could be*
> *1/3 cup dry white wine)*
> *basic seasonings: salt, black pepper*

The flour is cooked in the butter or oil—just a few minutes for white sauce, so that the flour is not raw tasting, and several minutes for brown sauce, so that the flour is well browned.

In the meantime, milk, water or stock is being heated—milk to scalding, water or stock to boiling.

When the flour has cooked sufficiently, remove the pan from the stove and wait for it to stop bubbling. Pour in the boiling or near-boiling liquid. Watch out for the steam! When it stops steaming, stir the mixture briskly with a whisk, a fork, or a spoon. Use a spoon or spatula to scrape out the corners of the pan so that all the flour-oil mixture is incorporated into the water. Then put it back on the heat and let the sauce simmer for several minutes. Season lightly with salt and pepper.

The butter or oil serves two purposes: dispersing and suspending the flour particles until they have cooked in the liquid, and adding body and flavor to the sauce. If you are not using oil, after the flour has roasted, add the liquid a quarter cup at a time, stirring.

Flavoring the Sauce

White and brown sauces can be flavored with vegetables, especially onion, garlic and mushrooms, with wine, lemon juice, and with a variety of herbs and spices. Go easy on the seasonings until you get a feel for how each thing flavors the sauce, and also a taste for the cumulative effect of the additions.

Herbs: Often one, can be two or more in combination: About 1/8 teaspoon—to taste!—thyme, sage, marjoram, oregano, basil, tarragon, chervil, dill, savory. A bay leaf can be put in the heating liquid.

    Spices: Often one, can be two or more in combination: About 1/8 teaspoon—to taste (start with less)—dry mustard, powdered ginger, cardamom, coriander, mace, nutmeg, fennel, anise.

    Wine: A tablespoon or more: Dry white wine, sherry, dry vermouth, brandy. Use as a seasoning, or (dry white wine especially) to replace some of the liquid in a brown sauce.

    Tang: A teaspoon or more: Lemon juice, lime juice, Worcestershire sauce.

    Vegetables: Dice and sauté: Onion, carrot, celery, green pepper before adding to the sauce. Sliced mushrooms, pressed garlic, tomato paste can be added without prior cooking.

    Cheese and cream: White sauces or brown sauces become *Cheese Sauces* with the addition of grated cheese, or *Cream Sauces* with the addition of cream. Add the grated cheese just before serving. Use up to an ounce of cheese to a cup of sauce. Since cheese has some salt in it, add only a little salt until the cheese has been added.

Some Specific Recipes & Variations

Herbed White Sauce: Put a bay leaf in heating milk. Season the thickened sauce with thyme, nutmeg, and garlic.

    Mushroom Sauce: Add a quarter pound of sliced mushrooms to the simmering sauce (brown or white) five minutes before serving. Season with lemon juice and minced onion.

    Mushroom Cheese Sauce: Season with brandy, dry vermouth, or sherry. Add the grated cheese as usual, just before serving.

    Cheese Sauces: Season with dry mustard, mace or nutmeg. Other seasonings for cheese sauces are garlic, Worcestershire sauce, powdered ginger, an herb.

Herbed Wine Sauce: Make one-third of the liquid in a brown sauce dry white wine. Season with rosemary, dill, tarragon, garlic, lemon juice, in addition to salt and pepper.

Tassajara Vegetable Sauce

We use this sauce with soybeans, using the bean cooking liquid in the sauce.

> *one cup of white sauce or brown sauce*
> *diced: ½ onion, ½ stalk celery, ½ carrot*
> *thyme, sage, parsley*

Make a white sauce or brown sauce following the Basic Recipe. Sauté the diced vegetables and add them to the simmering sauce. Season with thyme, sage and minced parsley.

Tassajara Brown Gravy

This is our favorite for mashed potatoes.

> *one cup of brown sauce, one diced onion, garlic, (freshly grated ginger,) soy sauce, salt (if needed), pepper, dark sesame oil (if available)*

Make the sauce according to the Basic Recipe, using whole wheat or barley flour if you have them and roasting the flour thoroughly—until well browned. Sauté the onion until golden brown and add it to the sauce. Season first with soy sauce and then with salt if necessary. Add the garlic, ginger, pepper to taste and, just before serving, a few drops of dark sesame oil.

One of the ways in which these sauces can be used is in baking. Precook grains, beans or potatoes completely. Sauté vegetables a few minutes before combining them with the sauce, and bake for twenty to thirty minutes in a 300° oven. Using this method, a dish can be prepared before the last-minute rush.

Although any number of combinations are possible, try:

—An *Herbed White Sauce* with vegetables, especially cauliflower, broccoli, green beans, asparagus.

—A *Mushroom Sauce* with grains.

—A *Cheese Sauce* with noodles.

As with salad dressings, the choice of a sauce depends not only on the dish it is to be used in, but also on the rest of the menu.

Cornstarch Thickened Sauces

Cornstarch is often used to thicken pies and fillings. It is also useful in thickening vegetable dishes which have excess liquid, including most Chinese vegetable dishes (that's the way they're made). Cornstarch is the finest version of corn flour, and cornstarch sauces are really just a special example of flour-thickened sauces. Other flours, or arrowroot, could be used in place of cornstarch in the following sauces. (Instructions for dissolving cornstarch are on page. 12.)

For Chinese-Style Vegetables

Season water or stock with soy sauce, salt, perhaps a little sherry or vinegar, and some pepper.

Sauté vegetables with freshly pressed garlic and freshly grated ginger (more can be added later) for three or four minutes.

Add the seasoned stock, cover, and simmer-steam until nearly tender, about five to eight minutes. Check the seasoning, then add dissolved cornstarch to thicken.

If some of the vegetables require longer cooking than the others, sauté them separately for a longer time, and then add them with the seasoned liquid. If some of the vegetables require less cooking (peas, spinach, tomato), add them five minutes before the end of cooking.

Sweet & Sour Sauce

A potent sauce for fried noodles or fried rice, eggplant, vegetable burgers. Use it sparingly.

> ¾ cup water or stock or tomato juice
> 3/8 cup sugar (honey or molasses or brown sugar)
> 1½ T cornstarch dissolved in ¼ cup cold water
> soy sauce, pepper or tabasco, garlic, ginger, dark sesame oil,
> worcestershire sauce.

Heat water with sugar and vinegar. When it is boiling, stir in the dissolved cornstarch. Season with soy sauce and pepper or Tabasco sauce. The other seasonings are optional.

Additions and Variations:

As usual, sautéed vegetables can be added. Cut the vegetables in small pieces or mince them. Sauté briefly in oil before adding to the

200

sauce. Add the vegetables either before or after thickening the sauce. Carrots, green peppers and pineapple chunks make excellent additions to sweet and sour sauces, as do onions.

Tomato Sauces

These are similar to tomato soups, only thicker. A tomato sauce could be made by thickening tomato soup with cornstarch, or by using tomato juice as the liquid in a brown sauce.

Here is the other way tomato sauces are made:

vegetables: onion, celery, peppers, mushroom, garlic
oil for sautéing: olive (if you have it)
tomatoes: fresh, or canned tomato juice, or tomato paste diluted
to taste
water as needed

Dice the vegetables and sauté them in oil. Add the garlic, the fresh or canned tomatoes—diced (or tomato juice, or tomato paste). Add water for the amount of sauce you want.

seasonings: salt, pepper
herbs: bay leaf, oregano, thyme, basil, parsley (rosemary,
cumin, sugar)

Season with salt and pepper, then moderately with herbs. Let it all simmer for half an hour or more. Check and adjust the seasoning before serving.

Tassajara Version:

We make this sauce with fork-size chunks of fresh-picked summer vegetables: green beans, zucchini, crookneck squash, eggplant, green peppers. Sauté them for five minutes and add to the sauce twenty minutes before serving.

—Dried mushrooms make a flavorful and chewy addition to tomato sauce.

—Other grated cheeses, besides Parmesan, can be colorful and tasty garnishings for tomato sauce.

Nut Sauces

These are a treat when served with grains, pastas or vegetables (especially those in the cabbage family which have a strong flavor). Nut sauces also make appropriate dressings for salads, especially noodle and grain. They are quite simple to make if you have a nut or seed butter to start with.

A Basic Recipe for Nut Sauce

vegetables: onion
½ cup nut butter: peanut, sesame, tahini, cashew, walnut, almond

Nut sauces don't have to be made with onions, but they're good that way. If using onion, dice it and sauté for five to ten minutes.

¾ cup water or stock (could be ¼ cup orange juice or 2 T lemon juice)

Thin the nut butter gradually with the liquid and add it to the onions. Simmer the mixture on low heat.

seasonings: salt, pepper, soy sauce, miso, vinegar, garlic, ginger, red pepper, cardamom, coriander, nutmeg, mace, cumin, thyme, sage

Season with salt and pepper. If seasoning with soy sauce and/or miso, omit the salt until you have added the soy. Nut sauces seem to welcome hot seasonings. They also welcome small amounts of the more peppery spices—cardamom, coriander, nutmeg or mace, and the pungent herbs—thyme or sage.

garnishings: parsley, watercress, pepper cress, green onion

Garnish with parsley, peppery cresses or green onion.

Notes:
　　—Whole or chopped nuts can be mixed in.
　　—Nut butters can also be used to flavor white or brown sauces.
　　—Sprouts, due to their moist freshness, are a complementary garnish for nut sauces, which tend to give a dry feeling.

Cream Cheese Sauces

This is one of the best and easiest of sauces. Cream cheese sauce makes onions, carrots and celery pass for something fancy, and its fairly mild flavor suits it to the more delicately flavored vegetables—asparagus, squashes, peas.

cream cheese or neufchatel cheese
small amount of liquid: hot water, warmed milk, vegetable
cooking liquid, lemon juice, dry white wine
seasonings: see the section on white and brown sauces

Soften the cream cheese or Neufchatel by mashing it with a fork or spoon. Gradually mix in the liquid to bring the cheese to a sauce consistency. Season, and that's it. Heat gently in a double boiler so that it doesn't boil or separate.

Serve with grains, noodles or vegetables, or add it to them for baked dishes.

Seasoned Butters

These can go on vegetables or grains, or French bread.

butter
seasonings: garlic, salt, (herbs); or lemon juice, salt, thyme;
or celery seed, poppy seed, sesame seed, salt; or whatever

Melt the butter. Season it. Taste with a piece of bread or vegetable. Minced onions or peppers can be cooked in the melted butter as part of the "sauce."

Honey Butter

This is one other butter which we use a great deal for pancakes.

About half butter and half honey, heated together. It can be seasoned with *orange rind.* Pancakes!

Main Dishes

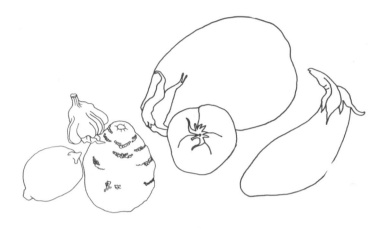

It doesn't take much to make a simple dish into a "main dish"—some protein, possibly eggs or cheese, and a good presentation. For instance, put heated, seasoned beans in a casserole with a layer of cheese on top, either grated or in a mandala of slices.

Or stuff the beans into some green peppers or tomatoes and bake (350°) for twenty to twenty-five minutes.

Mix the beans with some beaten egg and bake (350°) for twenty-five to thirty minutes. Or put the hot beans in a casserole, make some hollows in the surface, put an egg in each hollow and bake until the eggs cook—ten to fifteen minutes.

In a casserole, cover the beans with mixed, sautéed vegetables, bake to heat through or to keep hot. Sprinkle with nuts.

Or again, bake the beans with a nut sauce, sprinkle with parsley.

Just think, what will it take to make this dish a main dish? To make this meal complete? What will give strength and energy, full-bodied sustenance? Is that pea soup main enough? Or does it need celery, tomato chunks, seasoning, grated cheese? What should accompany it to make it complete? Garlic bread? Cheese there instead of in the soup?

What follows are casseroles, pies, stuffed pastries, stuffed vegetables, burgers, and so forth. But don't forget simple egg dishes, bean dishes, or rule out soups and salads.

Baked Vegetables

Vegetables can be baked with or without liquid—Vegetable Stew or Vegetable Bake. Accompanied by white or brown sauce (mushroom or cheese), baked vegetables make a hearty and satisfying main dish. Root vegetables are often preferred for baking and stewing, but many other vegetables can also be used. Here's how you go about it:

Outline for Baked Vegetables

Suggested Vegetables:
   longer cooking, one or more: onions, carrots, yams, potatoes, sweet potatoes, winter squashes, white radish (daikon), turnip, eggplant
   shorter cooking, one or more: summer squashes, celery, cauliflower, broccoli, cabbage, tomato, mushrooms

Wash vegetables and cut them in large pieces, perhaps quarters or sixths. (Mushrooms can be left whole.) Make enough pieces so that everybody will get some of everything.

   oil or butter; salt, pepper

Oil a baking dish and put in the longer-cooking vegetables. Baste generously with oil or butter (perhaps a seasoned butter or oil) and sprinkle with salt and pepper. Bake, covered, at 350° for sixty minutes. Baste several times during the baking, particularly if the dish is uncovered. Add the shorter-cooking vegetables for the last thirty minutes.

   For a stew: Add heated water, stock or sauce to the vegetables before baking, so that they are about half covered. Then cover and bake for about forty minutes, or until tender. Add shorter-cooking vegetables for the last thirty minutes.

   —Water or stock can be drained off after baking and made into a gravy by using it for the liquid in a brown sauce. Check the seasoning and serve.

   —Another way to make a vegetable bake or a vegetable stew is to sauté the vegetables for two to three minutes before putting them in the baking dish. This coats them with oil.

—For *dumplings,* add radish-size lumps of biscuit dough, or any of the doughs which come later in this section, such as Pie Dough or Knish Dough.

Miso Stew

> *6-8 inch strip of kombu*
> *carrots, onions, white radish (daikon), burdock root*
> *water or stock*
> *miso or soy sauce*
> *oil*

Use one carrot, burdock root, and onion per person. One large white radish for about four people. Boil the kombu in a few cups of water for ten minutes. Set the water aside. Slice the kombu, then fry it in oil and line the bottom of the stew pot with it. Cut the other vegetables in large pieces and put them into the top on top of the kombu. Season the kombu soaking water with miso or soy sauce, and pour it over the vegetables. Cover with a tight-fitting lid and bake for an hour or more at 350°.

To thicken the liquid, drain it off the vegetables, heat to boiling and thicken with cornstarch dissolved in cold water (see p. 12). Season with garlic or grated ginger if you like them, although the sauce should be quite flavorful already.

Variations:
—If you don't have kombu, omit it.
—Potatoes, eggplant, winter squashes, mushrooms, broccoli, cabbage, cauliflower and other vegetables are equally good with miso or soy sauce.
—Quicker-cooking vegetables such as broccoli, cabbage, cauliflower, green beans, peas, greens, can be added towards the end of the cooking. They'll be nicely done in twenty to thirty minutes.

Five Color Stew

To keep the colors five, cook the beets separately and add them at the last, without their cooking liquid. Use one of each root vegetable per person, and enough greens to go around.

beets, potatoes, onions, carrots, beet greens, oil, salt, pepper, water

Wash the vegetables and, except for the onions, leave the peels on. Cut them all in large chunks or sections. Cut the beet greens in one-inch pieces and set them aside. Place all the other vegetables in an oiled baking dish, baste with oil, and sprinkle with salt and pepper. Put a half cup of water or more in the bottom of the dish, cover, and bake for about forty-five minutes. Add the beet greens, cover again, and bake for another five minutes.

If this dish is cooked on top of the stove, it will take five to ten minutes less cooking time. Add more water if needed.

Variations:

(No longer five colors, but still tasty.)

—Substitute other vegetables: sweet potatoes for potatoes, winter squash for carrots, spinach for beet greens, mushrooms for beets.

—For *Eggplant Stew,* use eggplant (one for every three or four people), onion, green or red peppers, celery and pitted olives. Use a generous amount of olive oil to start with, and bake without water. Use wedges of tomato for added moisture. Season with garlic salt and pepper.

—For a *Tomato-Cabbage Stew,* use onions, celery, cabbage, green peppers (or corn) and tomatoes. Slice the vegetables and sauté them all for two to three minutes, except for the tomatoes. Mix everything, including tomatoes, together and season with salt, pepper, garlic and marjoram. Bake at 300° for about thirty minutes. Serve garnished with sliced hard-boiled eggs.

Making a Casserole

Casseroles are made in "casseroles"—oven-proof dishes which are also suitable for serving at the table. For several weeks when I was first cooking I made casseroles every day. They are excellent for using leftover, as well as fresh, foods. Topped with a layer of cheese, bread crumbs, chopped nuts or minced parsley, casseroles create an element of suspense and, hopefully, delighted anticipation as to what's inside of them. And the possibilities for what's inside are endless. Broadly speaking, anything cooked in a casserole (dish) will be a casserole, so the question is how is it done with each particular thing?

When starting with *grains* or *beans,* they should be already cooked.

Potatoes can be raw or precooked.

Vegetables, often put in after a light sautéing, are the least able to stand extra cooking time, so if they are precooked the other ingredients should be precooked, too.

Casseroles dry out as they bake, so the most important thing is to see that, one way or another, the casserole has plenty of moisture. This can come from water, soup, milk, egg with milk, sauce, vegetable juices or juicy vegetables, especially tomatoes.

Casseroles are assembled in two ways. One way is to mix everything together, adding moisture if necessary, season, and put in a greased dish, pot, or what have you. Smooth out the surface and then top with something. Bake. The casserole has the proper amount of moisture if it is slightly mushy, like (cooked) cereal.

The other way is to build up the casserole in layers. Usually grains, beans, pasta or potatoes are put on the bottom, so that they soak up the flavorful juices from above. On top of these comes a layer of vegetable(s), with possibly soup, sauce, tomatoes, or liquid added for the necessary moisture. Then it is topped as before.

A casserole can be made well in advance. If all or most of its ingredients are cold, the casserole will take an hour at 350° to get piping hot through and through. If its ingredients are hot already, the casserole can still easily stand twenty to thirty minutes in the oven. If it is to bake for more than twenty to thirty minutes, make sure that the casserole has plenty of moisture—those crisped noodles are awfully tough.

Especially if several dishes are being prepared, getting at least one of them into casserole form will allow more time and space to get the other things ready.

Basic Recipe for Casseroles

At least one cup of ingredients, other than liquid, per person.

Start with:
cooked grain: rice, cracked or bulgur wheat, barley, noodles, spaghetti, etc.
cooked beans: soy, lentils, white, kidney, etc.
cooked or semi-cooked vegetables: potato, onion, cabbage, eggplant, carrot, green beans, asparagus, etc.

Complement with:
any of the above, or onion, mushroom, tomato, celery, green pepper, nuts, dried fruit

Moisten with:
water, stock or cooking liquid, tomato sauce or slices or paste, milk (sour cream, yogurt), white sauce or brown sauce, egg-and-milk

Season with:
salt, pepper, herbs, spices, garlic

Add or top with:
grated cheese, bread crumbs, ricotta cheese

Onion, mushroom, celery, tomato, green peppers are often used for extra flavor.

Mix the liquid together with the assembled ingredients until they are the consistency of cooked cereal, or pour the liquid over the top of the layered ingredients. Top with grated cheese, bread crumbs, chopped nuts. Bake, covered, at 350° for one hour if the ingredients were cold, or for twenty to thirty minutes, or longer, if the ingredients were heated.

If topped with cheese, remove the lid for the final five or ten minutes to brown slightly. The casserole may be removed from the oven five to ten minutes before serving time—the dish will cool slightly while its contents remain hot.

Note: The specific recipes which follow are examples of different *types* of casseroles. By sticking with the type, but changing the ingredients, you can make these recipes become something quite different from what they start out as. Some possible transformations are suggested under the "variations."

Lentils With Onions & Peppers

(Serves 4)

3-4 cups cooked lentils, 2 onions, 4 oz. grated cheddar cheese, water or stock if needed

Slice or dice the onions and sauté them until they are transparent. Combine with the lentils and season with salt and pepper. Rinse out the pan used for frying the onions with a small amount of water and, if the beans are not moist enough, add this to them. Put the beans in a greased casserole dish and top with cheese. If the beans were cold, bake for an hour at 350°, covered except for the last five to ten minutes. If the beans were hot, they may be baked for a shorter time.

Variations:
   —In addition to onion, use one or more of these: celery, carrot, mushrooms, greens. Slice and sauté with the onions.
   —Use other kinds of cheese besides cheddar.
   —Add a layer of sliced tomatoes or seasoned tomato sauce on top of the bean and onion mixture. Top with cheese.
In place of lentils, use other precooked beans, cooked barley, rice, Bulgur wheat, sliced and cooked, or mashed, potatoes, green beans, asparagus, eggplant, summer or winter squash. If using summer squash, green beans, eggplant or asparagus, sauté or steam them briefly before adding to the casserole with onions. Bake for about thirty minutes.
   —May use 8-10 onions, omitting the beans and topping with tomatoes and cheese. Bake fifteen to thirty minutes to heat thoroughly.

Pilaf

(Serves 4)

2-3 cups cooked bulgur wheat (a cup or less dry), 1 onion, 1-2 stalks celery, ½ cup raisins, ½ cup nuts (almonds, walnuts, peanuts or cashews), water or stock as needed, seasonings (salt, pepper, thyme, coriander, cloves), topping (bread crumbs or chopped nuts)

Dice and sauté the onion and celery for three to four minutes and add them to the Bulgur wheat, along with the nuts and raisins. Add liquid to give the mixture a moist consistency. Season carefully to taste. Put in greased casserole and top with the bread crumbs or nuts. Bake up to one hour at 350° to heat thoroughly.

Variations:

—In place of Bulgur wheat, use precooked cracked wheat, white or brown rice, millet or part leftover cereal.

—In addition to, or in place of, the vegetables that are listed, use green pepper, carrot, green onion, peas, apple; sliced dates in place of raisins.

—Alternate seasonings are thyme, sage, garlic, rosemary, cinnamon. Or ginger and mace.

—Topping may be omitted, or it may be sliced oranges.

Try beans instead of Bulgur wheat, with onion, pepper, apple, carrot. Winter squash also likes this treatment.

—Try sweet potato with ingredients listed, or with pineapple, nuts, cinnamon, lemon peel.

—With regular potatoes, omit sweet items and use onion, peas, celery and nuts.

Potato-Bean Bake

(Serves 4)

> *1½ cups lentils, 1-2 cups mashed potatoes, 1½ cups soy beans,*
> *1 large onion, mushrooms, water or stock as needed,*
> *seasonings (salt, pepper, garlic, basil, oregano, parsley)*

Slice and sauté onions with garlic and mushrooms, using a sprinkling of herbs in the oil. Combine with the beans and mashed potatoes. Rinse out the frying pan with a half cup of water or stock and add this to the bean mixture (it should be fairly moist). Season carefully. Put in greased casserole dish and bake at 350° until thoroughly heated. Sprinkle with parsley before serving.

This casserole is a good example of how several *principal* ingredients can be combined.

Variations:

—In place of lentils, soy beans and potatoes, use other beans

and grains (leftovers, favorites, requests).
  —How about white beans with zucchini, spinach and garlic?
  —In place of potato, use mashed cooked eggplant.

You could use just lentils and soy beans with the onions on the
first night, add potatoes the second night, top with cheese the
third night, and have stuffed cabbage the fourth night.

Eggplant-Tomato Sauce Casserole

(Serves 4)

> *1 eggplant, 2-4 zucchini, olive oil; 2 cups tomato sauce with*
> *1 diced onion and 2 green peppers seasoned with garlic, basil,*
> *salt and pepper; ½ cup grated parmesan cheese*

Make the tomato sauce first: Sauté the onion and peppers, add
tomato chunks, sauce or paste diluted with water. Season with
salt, pepper, garlic and basil. (See p. 201 for other tomato sauces.)
Cut the eggplant and squash in large chunks or strips. Sauté in olive
oil for three to four minutes. Place in greased casserole. Top with
tomato sauce and grated cheese. Bake for an hour at 350°. May
be served hot or cold.

Variations:
  —In place of zucchini, use other summer squashes, carrots,
green beans, cabbage or sweet corn kernels.
  —Add mushrooms to the tomato sauce.
  —Use other seasonings: garlic, thyme and tarragon; parsley,
cumin and oregano.
  —Use other cheeses: cheddar, jack, Edam, Gouda, cottage,
ricotta, etc.

In place of, or in addition to, eggplant and zucchini, use noodles,
potatoes, grains, beans or stale bread cubes.

Poached Egg Casserole

(Serves 4)

This is very similar to the preceding casserole, but with a delightful
addition.

3 onions, 3 green peppers, ½ head of cabbage, 3 cloves garlic, 3-4 tomatoes, olive oil, salt and pepper, 4-6 eggs, ½ cup grated cheddar cheese

Slice or dice the onions and peppers, and cut the cabbage in thin shreds. Cut the tomatoes in wedges or slices. Start the onions frying in the olive oil with garlic, then add the peppers and cabbage. When these have softened, add the tomatoes and cover; cook gently for several minutes. Season and place in greased casserole. Make four to six hollows in the surface and break an egg into each. Sprinkle with cheese and bake until the eggs set, about ten to fifteen minutes. Be sure that the other ingredients are hot before baking, since they won't heat through in the time it takes for the eggs to set. If you make this casserole ahead of time, heat in the oven for thirty to forty minutes before adding the eggs and cheese.

Variations:
—Other vegetables can be used in place of, or in addition to, the onions, peppers and cabbage: green beans, peas, carrots, asparagus, greens. Cut them finely and add to the sauté.
—Tomato sauce can be used in place of tomatoes.

The eggs could go in hollows of precooked spaghetti, noodles, grains, beans.

Rice with Cheese & Milk

(Serves 4)

2 cups milk, 2 cups cooked rice, 2 cups grated cheddar cheese, salt and pepper

Heat the milk to scalding and mix it with the rice. Season and place in greased casserole. Top with cheese and bake, covered, for thirty-five to forty minutes, then bake uncovered for another five to ten minutes.

Variations:
—Use 1½ cups milk and 1½ cups cooked cereal in place of the 2 cups milk.
—A layer of vegetables could top the rice and milk before the cheese is added: sautéed onions and mushrooms, leftover vegetables.

—Use part milk and part ricotta cheese, cottage cheese, yogurt, sour cream, cream cheese or cream.

—Season with garlic, parsley, marjoram, basil, thyme or oregano, or with dry mustard or nutmeg.

Rice absorbs a lot of liquid. If using something which does not absorb as much liquid, use less milk. For instance:

—Sliced raw potatoes can be used. Use one medium potato per person. Slice and layer in casserole with sautéed onion and some of the grated cheese, sprinkling salt and pepper on each layer. Pour on the heated milk and top with the remainder of the cheese. The milk should cover just over half the potatoes. Bake, covered, at 400° for forty minutes.

—In place of rice, use another cooked grain, or noodles.

Sauced Potato Casserole

(Serves 4)

4 medium potatoes, 2 onions, 2 cups seasoned white sauce (p. 196)
½ cup cheddar cheese (grated), green onion for garnish

Cut the potatoes into thick rounds or chunks. Section the onions. Place in greased casserole and pour the white sauce over. Cover and bake at 350° for forty to fifty minutes, or until the potatoes are tender. Uncover, add the cheese, and bake five minutes longer. Sprinkle with sliced green onion and serve.

Variations:
—Use a brown sauce or nut sauce.
—May be garnished with chopped, pitted olives.
—Sprinkle with paprika.

In place of raw potato, use mashed potato, sweet potato, cooked grains, beans, noodles, spinach, broccoli, cauliflower, celery, carrots, green beans, asparagus, mushrooms. If using spinach or other greens, wilt them in boiling salted water first, then cut finely and place in casserole with the onions. Most vegetables, other than potatoes, will only need to bake for about thirty minutes.

—Just onions could be used—about 8-10 of them.

Bulgur-Tahini Casserole

(Serves 4)

3 cups cooked bulgur wheat (about 1 cup dry), 1 onion (diced), 2 cloves garlic, 1/3 cup tahini (or peanut butter), ½ t salt, 2 eggs (beaten), ¼ cup milk

Sauté the onion with the garlic until translucent—or longer, until browned. Mix onions with the remaining ingredients and put in a greased casserole. If the wheat was hot to start with, bake for twenty minutes at 350°. If it was cold, bake fifty to sixty minutes or until thoroughly heated.

Variations:
   —Add grated cheese, mixed in or on top.
   —Use stock or tomato juice in place of the milk.
   —Omit eggs and add more liquid.
   —Use grated potato, grated carrot, diced onion. Check after thirty minutes of baking.
   —In place of, or in addition to, onion, use leeks, green peppers, peas, tomatoes, or celery and carrot. Add these vegetables either finely cut (grated) or sautéed first.

In place of Bulgur wheat, use cooked rice, barley, millet, buck-wheat, cooked beans, or a vegetable: asparagus, green beans, broccoli, cauliflower, spinach or chard.
   —Use sliced or mashed potatoes in place of the Bulgur wheat.
   —This recipe is quite similar to a quiche (see p. 219), except that there is less egg and milk in proportion to the other ingredients. Therefore, the egg and milk make an inconspicuous background, while in a quiche they form a more prominent base for vegetables or other ingredients. Adding one or two more eggs, and two or three times as much milk, will make a very quiche-like casserole.

Cabbage Casserole

(Serves 4)

1 head cabbage, 1 to 2 cups ricotta cheese, 1 or 2 eggs, tomato sauce, a little milk if needed, grated cheese, oil (olive or corn) or butter, salt, pepper, garlic

Cut up cabbage and sauté in oil with salt, pepper and garlic. Cook until the cabbage is limp. (Maybe sprinkle on a little white wine.) Mix ricotta with eggs and milk until creamy. Season with salt and pepper to taste (garlic powder optional). Make a tomato sauce (see p. 201). Layer the casserole dish first with cabbage, then the ricotta mixture, then tomato sauce. Usually there is enough to do this three times, ending with the tomato sauce. Bake at 350° for about half an hour, then sprinkle on a little grated cheese (mozzarella, cheddar, Parmesan) and bake for an additional five minutes.

Variations:
   —In place of ricotta cheese, use cottage cheese or grated cheese, with or without the egg and milk. (The tomato sauce should provide plenty of liquid.)
   —Use sliced tomatoes in place of tomato sauce. (Cabbage, grated cheddar, sliced tomatoes and seasoning is simple and delicious.)
   —Especially if using sliced tomatoes in place of tomato sauce, add layers of vegetables: sautéed onions, sliced mushrooms, a peeled and diced cucumber. Layer on top of the cabbage or in between layers of cabbage.

In place of cabbage, use cauliflower leaves, collard greens, spinach, chard, eggplant, summer squashes, broccoli, cauliflower, asparagus, green beans. Cook the tougher greens in boiling water for two to three minutes rather than sautéing.
   —In place of cabbage, use lasagne noodles or other pasta. Cook them until just tender and toss with olive oil before completing dish.

Baked Eggplant Moussaka

(Serves 6-8)

Here's a casserole which combines several of the possibilities presented in the preceding recipes. It is very rich.

   large eggplant, salt

Cut the eggplant in half-inch slices. Sprinkle on salt and let stand for twenty minutes. Drain off liquid which has accumulated. Bake the eggplant slices on a greased cookie sheet for ten minutes at 350°.

2 onions (diced), 3 cloves garlic, ½ cup olive oil, ½ cup butter

Sauté the onions and garlic in *some* of the oil and butter.

½ cup tomato sauce, ½ cup wine, ½ cup parsley, 1 lb. grated jack cheese

Add the parsley, tomato sauce and wine. When heated, remove from the stove and gradually add the grated cheese.

Grease a large casserole or cake pan. Sandwich the filling between layers of eggplant which have been brushed with the oil-butter mixture.

2 cups white sauce (see p. 196), 4 eggs, beaten

Prepare a white sauce and beat it gradually into the already beaten eggs. Pour over the eggplant.

1 cup grated parmesan, ¼ t cinnamon

Brush the top with remaining oil-butter mixture and sprinkle with grated Parmesan cheese and cinnamon. Bake at 350° for one hour.

Variations:

—Use other fillings, other sauces. For instance, the eggplant could be layered with seasoned lentils, topped with a nut sauce.

In place of eggplant, use lasagne noodles, potatoes, zucchini or cabbage.

Baked Eggs

(Serves 6)

Here is a "casserole" made just with "moistening." It is not far from a soufflé, but much easier to make.

6 eggs, 1 cup milk, 1 T flour, salt and pepper

Separate the eggs. Whip the whites until they are stiff. Beat the yolks with the milk, flour, salt and pepper. Fold in most of the whites, and turn into a greased pie tin or casserole dish. Bake until the eggs are set, about twenty minutes at 350°. Add the remaining whites and return to the oven until browned slightly. This is an excellent way to serve hot eggs to many people all at once.

Variations:
  —Add a half cup or more grated cheese to the yolks.
  —Layer the bottom of the casserole with fried vegetables: mushrooms, zucchini, broccoli, others.
  —Season with basil, thyme or tarragon.
  —Sweeten with strawberry preserves. (Hold the broccoli . . . or would that be a new taste sensation?)

Main Dish Pies

Pies make elegant main dishes, but they can be presented less elegantly—without the crust—and be called casseroles. In fact, a main dish pie could be considered a casserole bottomed with pie dough instead of the more usual rice, potatoes or noodles. To make a pie is to make a special effort to please, to encourage people. Here's a pie crust:

Half & Half Pie Crust

Half white and half whole wheat flour, half butter and half oil. For two medium-sized pies.

> *1 cup whole wheat flour, 1 cup white flour, ¼ t salt,*
> *1/3 cup butter, 1/3 cup corn oil, 5-6 T cold (ice) water*

Sift flours and salt together. Cut in the butter. While stirring with a fork, add the oil, and then the water a little at a time. Tossing like a salad, by hand, mix quickly into a ball. If it doesn't quite shape up, add a little more water. Divide in two. Roll out on a floured surface with a floured rolling pin till ¼ inch thick, and place in two pie tins without stretching the dough too much. Flute the edges. Make fork marks on the bottom and sides, brush with beaten egg if you like, and bake for five to ten minutes at 375°, unless a recipe calls for a *fully* baked crust.

  This dough is easy to handle. All whole wheat or all white flour doughs are more difficult to handle, and white flour pie dough usually needs refrigeration for an hour before using.

218

Variations:

—One cup whole wheat and one cup white flour, with ½ cup butter and 1/6 cup oil is good too.

—Small amounts (½ cup) of other flours could be used with ½ cup whole wheat and one cup white.

—Margarine or shortening can be used in place of butter.

—Ground nuts can be added. Combine first with the oil.

—May be seasoned with thyme or sage.

Here are three general ways to make a pie. 1) vegetables and/or cheese baked in eggs and milk (quiche), 2) cooked vegetables with sauce, 3) and cheese pie.

Basic Quiche Recipe

choice of sliced or diced: yellow or purple onion, 1-2 leeks, several green onions
1 lb. sliced vegetables: mushrooms, spinach, chard, cauliflower, broccoli, squash
seasoning: salt, pepper, lemon juice, basil

Cook the onions in butter or oil for a couple of minutes. Stir in the rest of the sliced vegetables along with a sprinkling of salt, and possibly lemon juice or other seasoning. Cook, covered, over moderate heat until the vegetables have softened slightly and have begun to release their moisture—about five minutes. Uncover and turn up the heat to boil off some of the excess liquid (the rest can go in with the eggs and milk).

egg mixture: 3 eggs, 1 cup milk (all or partly cream, thinned cream cheese, ricotta or cottage cheese)
seasoning: nutmeg, pepper
grated cheese, up to ¼ lb.: usually swiss, could be cheddar, jack, parmesan, etc.

Beat the eggs with the milk, adding a dash of nutmeg and pepper. Mix in the vegetables, then pour into partially baked pie shell. Top with cheese. Bake, in the upper part of the oven, at 350° for thirty to forty minutes, or until puffed and browned.

Here is a specific example.

Mushroom Quiche

*1 onion (sliced), 1 lb. mushrooms, salt, pepper, 1 t lemon juice,
2 T port wine or sherry*

Sauté the onion in butter or oil for a couple of minutes. Add the
sliced mushrooms and season with salt, pepper, lemon juice and
wine. Add garlic if you wish. Cook, covered, over moderate heat
for five minutes. Then uncover and raise the heat to boil off some
of the excess liquid.

*3 eggs, 1 cup milk, 1/8-1/4 t nutmeg, pepper, 2 oz. grated swiss
cheese, 1 oz. grated parmesan cheese*

Beat the eggs and milk together with their seasoning. Stir in the
vegetables and their juices. Pour everything into a partially baked
pie shell, top with cheese, and bake at 350° until slightly browned
on top—thirty to forty minutes.

Variations:
—Remember that for an extra-hearty quiche you can use thinned
cream cheese, ricotta cheese, or cream in place of the milk.
—Other seasonings can be used, especially ginger, dry mustard.

Use other vegetables in place of the mushrooms: chard, spinach,
broccoli, cauliflower, cabbage, squashes, celery, green pepper,
carrots, peas—any vegetable. When using chard, spinach or collard
greens, drop the greens briefly into boiling salted water until they
become soft. Once they are drained, clump them together and
slice them, including the stalks, thinly.

More Quiche Variations of Special Interest:
—*Tassajara Quiche:* In addition to onions and another vegetable,
use 1½-2 doz. well-roasted almonds. Garnish with several snow peas,
along with cheese, before baking.
—*Cheese Quiche:* Omit the vegetables entirely, add another egg
and use ½ lb. or more grated cheese (one kind or a combination).
Bake fifteen minutes at 400°, then ten to fifteen minutes at 300°.

—*Gruel Quiche:* This is one of the easiest and best things to do with leftovers. A quiche can be made by adding the eggs and milk to almost any combination of leftovers, including grains, beans, noodles, spaghetti, vegetables.

Spoonbread

Here's a grain quiche without a crust.

½ cup hominy grits, 2 cups boiling water, 1 cup corn meal, 4 beaten eggs, 2 cups milk, ½ t baking powder, 1 T or more butter or oil

Start the grits cooking in boiling water, then continue cooking in a double boiler or over low heat for half an hour. Mix in the remaining ingredients. Put in a buttered casserole and bake for an hour at 350°. Serve with butter and a fork.

Variations:
—Use about 1½ cups of any cooked grain or cereal in place of the grits.
　—Add other uncooked cereals in place of the corn meal.
　—Add onions, mushrooms or vegetables.
　Mix in a little cheese.

Vegetable Pies

Here's a sample recipe.

1 onion, ¼ head of cabbage, 1 turnip, 2 small potatoes, 1 carrot; salt and pepper, 2 cloves garlic, thyme, basil, tarragon, 2 t whole dill seed (optional); 1 cup white sauce (see p. 196); large prebaked pie shell

Cut all the vegetables thinly into a variety of shapes. Sauté the onion, then add the potato, turnip and carrot. Add a little water, cover, and steam. In five minutes add the cabbage and the seasonings. Continue steaming another five minutes, or until the vegetables are tender. Combine the vegetables with a cup of white sauce and place in a *fully baked* pie shell. Bake briefly to heat or to keep hot if necessary.

Variations:

　—For vegetables, use onion, carrot, 6-12 dried mushrooms, sliced water chestnuts. Combine with a brown sauce seasoned with soy sauce, ginger, sherry.

　—Top with cheese and sliced tomatoes, dot with butter.

　—Sprinkle on top: wheat germ; toasted nuts; toasted sesame seeds, or poppy seeds.

　—Add ¼ cup prepared seaweed, or 1 sheet of nori, roasted and scissor-cut into small pieces (p. 105).

　—Use sliced tomatoes or a tomato sauce in place of the white sauce.

Cheese Pie

*1 onion, 1 stalk celery, small carrot, 6 oz. grated cheese,
½ cup rolled oats, ¼ cup melted butter or margarine, salt,
pepper, ½ t dry mustard, parsley or green onion for
garnishing*

Dice the vegetables and sauté them, starting with the onion. When they have begun to soften, remove them from the pan and combine with the remaining ingredients, seasoning to taste. Place in a partially baked pie shell and bake for twenty minutes at 375°. Garnish and serve.

Variations:

　—Use other vegetables.

　—Season with garlic, oregano or marjoram.

　—Omit rolled oats and add an egg.

Stuffed Vegetables & Pastries

This is a delightful, and time-consuming, way of presenting food which might otherwise pass for "the same old thing." Vegetables which can be stuffed include: artichokes, onions, tomatoes, large summer squashes, winter squashes, eggplant, green peppers, mushrooms, cabbage, chard, beets. Pastries to be stuffed include crêpes, popovers, knishes, empanadas and piroshki, as well as biscuit or bread dough.

How to prepare the vegetables and make the pastries comes first; how to concoct a stuffing comes next.

Vegetables Which Can Be Stuffed

Stuffed vegetables are usually baked, covered, in a small amount of water or stock. The stuffing should be fairly well heated at the outset since vegetables are only baked thirty minutes or less after stuffing. If without an oven, heat the stuffed vegetables, placed in a small amount of water and covered, on top of the stove.

Artichokes

Cut off the stem flush with the base of the artichoke and cut off the top third of the leaves, then, spreading the leaves apart, wash the artichokes. Turn upside down on a cutting board and press down to further open the leaves. Remove the yellow leaves from the center of the artichoke. Use a sturdy spoon to scrape out the fuzzy portion of the heart at the base. Sprinkle with lemon juice to prevent discoloring. Fit the artichokes snugly together in an inch of water, cover, and simmer-steam for about thirty minutes, or until nearly tender.

The artichokes are now ready for stuffing. The stems can be peeled and cooked for use in the stuffing. After stuffing, brush the artichokes with oil, place in a baking dish with an inch of water, cover and bake for thirty to forty-five minutes at 350°.

Beets

Steam, bake, or pressure cook whole beets. When tender, scoop out the insides, leaving a shell to be stuffed. Mash the insides and mix with the stuffing, say cheese, garlic, salt and pepper. Stuff and bake to heat thoroughly.

Cabbage & Chard

Wash and core a head of cabbage, then simmer in water or soup stock for five minutes. Carefully peel off the outer leaves and simmer the rest of the head again if the inside leaves are not pliable. Save the stock.

Arrange a big leaf with a little leaf in the middle. Put the stuffing on the little leaf, fold in the sides of the big leaf, fold the stem onto the top, then roll into a cylinder. Place in a baking pan with the loose flap on the bottom. Pour some of the cabbage water, tomato sauce, or an onion-mushroom brown sauce made with the cabbage water, over the rolls. Bake covered at 350° until heated— about thirty minutes. Garnish with freshly chopped parsley.

Simmer *Chard Leaves* until wilted. Cut off the stalks and save them for future use. Stuff like cabbage.

Eggplant

Here is one way to prepare eggplant for stuffing. Cut an eggplant in half lengthwise and make deep slits in the flesh. Sprinkle salt into these slits and let sit for half an hour or more. After pouring off the accumulated liquid, place the eggplant flesh side down in a quarter inch of water and bake in the oven at 350° for thirty minutes, or simmer, covered, on top of the stove for twenty minutes. Carefully scoop out the pulp, leaving half an inch of shell. Use the scooped-out pulp in the stuffing (onion, mushroom, tomato, seasoned lentils?). Brush the shell with butter or olive oil, stuff, and bake to heat thoroughly—350° for thirty minutes or longer.

Green Peppers

Wash the peppers, cut off the tops, remove the seeds and pith. The top can be saved to be put back on, or it can be cut up and put in the stuffing. Brush the inside of the shell with oil and sprinkle with salt, pepper and seasonings. After stuffing, bake for about thirty minutes at 350°.

Mushrooms

Use big ones if available—three, four or five inches! Clean the mushrooms and cut off the stems, leaving just enough so that a hole doesn't result. Dice the stems for use in the stuffing. Sauté the mushroom caps for a minute or two, face down in a generous amount of butter. When softened a little, turn them over and sprinkle each with salt, pepper, a little sugar, garlic powder—unless you sautéed garlic in the butter—a careful drop of Tabasco, generous drops of sherry, and herbs. Stuff the mushrooms, cover, and steam gently to heat. Lift out carefully, keeping in the juices. Stuffed mushrooms might be served on a platter of grain with a sauce.

Onions

Wash the onions and bake them in their skins at 350° for twenty-five to thirty minutes. Remove the skins and cut a slice off the top (opposite end from the root hairs). Cut off the root hairs so that the onion has a flat bottom to sit on. Remove most of the inside, leaving two or three layers of onion. Use the center portion on the stuffing (with, say, grated cheese, nuts and an egg or two). Stuff the onions and bake at 350° until they are fork piercing tender—about thirty minutes.

Squashes

If they are the long, slender kind, like a large zucchini, cut them in half lengthwise and scoop out the softish inner pulp. If they are the round, winter kind, cut off the top as you would when making a jack-o-lantern. Scoop out the seeds. Both summer and winter squashes should be precooked before they are stuffed, either steamed on top of the stove, or baked in the oven. Brush them generously with seasoned oil and/or butter. Steam summer squashes five to fifteen minutes, and steam winter squashes for twenty minutes, or bake for forty to fifty minutes. Stuff, then bake to thoroughly heat and finish the cooking—350° for about thirty minutes.

Tomatoes

Cut off the tops of the tomatoes, then carefully cut loose the pulp and scoop it out. Brush the interior with olive oil and sprinkle with salt, pepper and herbs. Once stuffed, arrange the tomatoes in a baking dish and bake in a moderate oven for twenty to twenty-five minutes.

Pastries for Stuffing

Here are some doughs which can be stuffed.

Crepes

1 cup flour, 1 cup milk, 4 eggs, ½ cup melted butter, (2-3 t white sugar,) (1-2 T brandy or rum)

Beat the ingredients until completely smooth. The batter should be very thin. It will be easier to handle if it is refrigerated for a half hour or more. Heat and butter a frying pan.

For a five or six inch frying pan, use about 2½-3 T of batter. As you pour in the batter (all at once), tilt the frying pan to spread it around before it cooks. Brown for about a minute on each side. After the first one or two crêpes, they won't stick as much, and little butter will be necessary. The crêpes may be used right away or stacked up for later use.

Roll up the crêpes with a couple tablespoons of stuffing. Place side by side in a pan. Sprinkle with Parmesan cheese and bake twenty minutes at 350°.

Knishes

2 cups flour, 1 t baking powder, salt and pepper, 3 eggs, 6 T oil, 1 egg, beaten

Sift the flour, baking powder and salt together. Make a well in the center, drop in the unbeaten eggs and oil, and begin mixing. If you see that there is not enough moisture, add some water. Knead the dough to make it smooth. Roll it out quite thinly. Cut out circles with a cup or bowl. Put a stuffing in the center of each circle and fold up the edges. Brush with beaten egg and bake at 350° until browned.

I have often made these like *Bear Claws*. Roll out strips of dough about 5-6 inches wide and 7-8 inches long. Put the stuffing down the middle, and fold the dough over the stuffing so that there is a half inch of overlap. Press the overlapping dough together. After placing the strip on a baking sheet, slash the top every couple of inches, and make cuts in the overlap to form the claws.

Piroshki

Sour Cream Pastry

1¾ cups sifted flour, ¼ cup butter, ½ t baking powder, 1 egg, ½ t salt, ½ cup thick sour cream or yogurt

Sift the flour with baking powder and salt. Cut in the butter. Beat the eggs lightly and mix with sour cream. Add the flour and mix lightly with a fork to combine. Knead it several times to get it smooth, but not so much that it gets stiff.

I make *Turnovers* with either this dough or with pie dough. Roll out a portion of the dough and cut it into 3 or 4 inch squares. Put some stuffing in the center of the square and fold the dough in half so that it forms a triangle. Then to seal, make twists at intervals around the edges. Bake for fifteen to twenty minutes at 350°, or until browned. (Pie dough turnovers can be browned on both sides in a skillet.)

Stuffings for Vegetables or Pastries

Stuffings are a wonderful way to use a wide assortment of foods, especially leftovers. The little bit of spinach or the stale heel of a loaf of bread may be just what's called for. And if you don't have what's called for, use something else. Stuffings are for playing, experimenting, tasting as you go along.

Keeping combinations simple is more likely to succeed than hastily throwing all sorts of things together, although that too can work. Feel it out. Try to get the stuffing right before it goes so far wrong that every addition just makes it worse.

Outline For Making Stuffings

Basis—one or more:
   pulp from vegetables to be stuffed
   mushrooms
   grains: rice, cracked wheat, bulgur wheat, buckwheat, corn
   kernels, wheat germ or bran
   beans: lentils, pintos, kidney, etc.
   vegetables: onion, carrot, spinach, tomatoes, any!
   bread cubes or crumbs
   cheese: grated, cottage, cream cheese, bleu cheese, parmesan
   hard-cooked eggs, chopped
   nuts, avocado, olives

There are a lot of things to choose from here, but chances are they won't all be present in your kitchen at once. The easiest thing is to see what needs to be used—in the refrigerator, the pantry, the bread box. Is there stale bread? Cooked grain? Beans? Vegetables? Start with what's there rather than trying to think something up. What's there will give you ideas.

Another thing to consider is what is being stuffed. A grain or bread cube stuffing is probably better in a vegetable than a pie dough, while pastries usually call for a vegetable, cheese or egg stuffing.

Next, what needs to be done to make it into a stuffing? Here are two factors (qualities) to consider:

Texture: Generally best if everything in the stuffing is cut or chopped into small pieces.

Consistency: Moist, but not runny. Grains and bread cubes can absorb some moisture. A stuffing can also be thickened with flour.

Moisten with:
   sour cream, yogurt, tomatoes, eggs, sauce, apple sauce, lemon
   juice or vinegar, melted butter, soy sauce, honey or molasses
Season with: choice of
   salt, pepper, garlic, soy sauce; herbs—parsley, oregano, rosemary;
   mint, curry powder

Most of the moisteners will also contribute to the seasoning when added.

Eggs are both a moistener and a thickener. When the eggs bake they thicken and absorb, but are still moist.

Other additions: These are not strictly necessary, especially in a straightforward cheese or mushroom stuffing, but in many cases they help.

celery, onion, green pepper, apples
raisins, sunflower seeds

The recipes which follow are a lot like the preceding casserole recipes, and often a leftover casserole can be the basis for a stuffing. Leftover stuffing can be baked with the stuffed vegetables or pastries, surrounding them or in a separate casserole dish.

Note: Here are some suggestions for stuffings which have gotten out of hand:

—Season the stuffing with tumeric, red pepper, or curry powder, and top with grated coconut.

—Season with sautéed onions, garlic and soy sauce.

—Add grated cheese.

Vegetable Stuffing

Cooked vegetables, moistened with wine, stiffened with bread crumbs.

1 onion, 1 green pepper, 2 tomatoes, 1 apple, ½ cup chopped nuts, 2 T dry wine or 1 T lemon juice, salt and pepper, bread crumbs

Dice all the vegetables and the apple. Sauté the onion and peppers in oil until the onion becomes transparent. Add the remaining ingredients and season to taste, while cooking over a moderate flame. Add bread crumbs until the mixture holds together. Check seasoning.

This stuffing can go in either pastries or vegetables.

Variations:

—Use cooked rice, cracked wheat or bread cubes for thickening, in place of the crumbs.

—Add cooked chopped greens—spinach, cabbage, chard—in place of, or in addition to, green pepper.

229

—In place of apple, use peaches, apricots, raisins, etc.

—Add chopped parsley, watercress or green onion.

—Fruit can be omitted.

—Other ingredients can replace those listed: celery, carrots, nuts; onion, eggplant, squash; onion, garlic, nuts.

—Sprinkling flour on the cooking vegetables will help take up the excess moisture.

—Make a sweet and sour stuffing by adding honey and (more) lemon juice to taste. Pineapple could be used in place of the apple.

Cottage Cheese Stuffing

The background here is cottage, cream or grated cheese, with an egg and possibly some sautéed vegetables in front.

1 lb. cottage cheese, 1 egg, salt, pepper, lemon juice, sugar, cinnamon

Season the cottage cheese and mix in the egg. This stuffing can be used in crêpes or vegetables.

Variations:

—Use cream cheese or grated cheese in place of the cottage cheese.

—If you want something to chew on, add chopped nuts or olives.

—Add vegetable pulp (cooked) which has been removed to make room for stuffing.

—Add leftover vegetables, drained and chopped.

—Add diced, sautéed onions, celery, mushrooms.

—Egg may be omitted.

—Season with nutmeg, ginger, dry mustard or garlic.

—Season with sweet basil, tarragon.

Mushroom Stuffing

Mushrooms and some other odds and ends, with a choice of thickening.

1 onion (diced), 1-3 cloves garlic, 2 tomatoes

½ lb. mushrooms, diced (or just the stems from mushrooms to be stuffed)
(cornstarch or arrowroot)
¼-½ cup grated parmesan cheese
salt, pepper, sugar, marjoram

Sauté the onion and garlic for several minutes, then add the mushrooms and tomato. Cook over moderate heat for a few minutes while you do some tentative seasoning (easy on the salt—the cheese is yet to come). Either let the liquid evaporate, or thicken with cornstarch (see p. 12). Add the grated cheese and check the seasoning.

This stuffing can also be thickened with the addition of bread crumbs or cubes, rice or other grain.

Cream cheese could also take up some of the moisture. First soften the cream cheese in a separate bowl by gradually adding liquid from the pan.

This is a good stuffing for either pastries or vegetables.

Variations:

—Use dried mushrooms (they really do the trick). Start with an ounce or so dry weight (see p. 52).

—Tomato may be omitted.

—Add other sautéed, diced vegetables, or chopped leftover vegetables.

—Cheese may be omitted—or use another kind.

—Add chopped olives or chopped hard-boiled eggs.

—Other ways to season: parsley, tarragon; soy sauce in place of salt.

Cheese Stuffings

These are easy, and have many uses.

2 cups assorted cheese, grated: 1 cup port salut, ¾ cup muenster,
¼ cup provolone
1/3 cup finely chopped sorrel or wild dock
2 cloves garlic, crushed
1 T freshly minced onion, 1 t dry onion

Combine the ingredients. Use for stuffing vegetables or pastries.

Another way to use this stuffing is to spread it between two layers of Pie Dough or Knish Dough. Use a ravioli rolling pin to divide it into squares, or place chopsticks at intervals and roll with an ordinary rolling pin (or bottle), forming deep grooves. Then place the chopsticks at right angles to these grooves and repeat the rolling. Cut into pieces with three or four little squares each. Bake on a cookie sheet for about thirty minutes at 375°, or until browned.

Variations:
—Use chard, spinach, chopped green onion or parsley, in place of the sorrel.
—Add diced, sautéed onion and celery.
—Use other cheese. A small amount of bleu cheese adds a great deal of flavor.
—Season with dry mustard, oregano or basil.
—Another way to think about using this recipe: add the cheese and seasoning to the scooped-out pulp of the vegetables that are being stuffed.

Bread-Cube Stuffing (Grain Stuffing)

The bread cubes need moistening, vegetables and seasoning to keep them company.

2 cups fresh or stale bread, cut into cubes
1 onion, diced; 1 celery stalk, sliced thinly
½ cup dried mushrooms, soaked and cut into thin strips
(save the soaking water)
½ cup minced parsley
seasoning: garlic, sage, thyme, rosemary
½ cup walnuts, chopped but not too finely

Sauté the onion with garlic. After a minute, add the celery and continue sautéing. In another minute or two, add the mushrooms, bread cubes, parsley and seasonings. If moisture is needed to hold everything together, add some of the mushroom soaking liquid. After the cooking is finished, add the walnuts.

Let the stuffing sit overnight for flavor-mellowing if you have a chance.

This is good for stuffing cabbage, chard, or other vegetables.

Variations:

—In place of dried mushrooms, use regular mushrooms.

—Use other vegetable combinations: onion and tomato, green pepper and carrot.

—Add chopped olives.

—Skip or alter herb seasoning.

In place of bread cubes, you can use bread crumbs, cooked rice, buckwheat groats, Bulgur wheat, other cooked grains, possibly cereal.

—If using rice in place of bread cubes, add some raisins, currants, or sliced dates. In place of the rosemary, season with a dash of cinnamon or cloves.

Chopped Egg Stuffing

3 hard-boiled eggs, chopped; 1 onion, 6 carrots, butter or oil, salt, pepper, 2 T sour cream or yogurt

Dice the onion and grate the carrots. Stir-fry them in the butter or oil for about five minutes, or until they are hot and limp. Season with salt and pepper, and possibly a touch of lemon juice or vinegar. Let the vegetable mixture cool, add the chopped eggs, moisten with sour cream, and check the seasoning. This stuffing can be used with either pastries or vegetables.

Variations:

—The vegetables can be cooked until they are soft and then mashed for a smooth-textured stuffing.

—Other vegetables can be used. Add chopped cooked greens, cabbage, celery, green beans, and so forth.

—Chopped nuts could be added.

Burgers

I don't make these often, but they can be an excellent main dish.

Basic Recipe for Burgers

Foundation: (one or more)
  cooked, ground soybeans; cooked oatmeal (thick); sunflower seed meal; grated raw potato; cooked lentils; cooked barley or rice

Burgers can often be started with leftovers. The first step is to grind, mash, or grate the basic ingredient. Whole grains need not be ground or mashed, as they add a marvelous chewy quality, barley especially.

Vegetable additions:
  onion, celery, carrot

The vegetable additions can either be grated or sautéed before being added.

Moistening:
  eggs

Eggs moisten and bind the ingredients together.

Thickening:
  bread crumbs, flour, wheat bran, wheat germ, dry oatmeal

These add bulk and thicken. Use eggs and thickening agents as necessary to make a mixture which can be shaped into patties—either by hand or with a couple of spatulas, large spoons, or rice paddles.

Seasoning:
  salt, pepper, parsley, garlic, thyme, sage, others

Season with salt and pepper. Use garlic, parsley and other herbs if you wish.
    If it makes the patties easier to handle, dust them with flour. (If they are particularly moist, you may just drop them by spoon into a frying pan.) Fry in oil over moderate heat until well browned on both sides. Serve with Tomato Sauce, White Sauce, or other.

Potato Cakes

4 medium potatoes (raw), 2 T wheat bran or wheat germ,
1 egg, salt and pepper, grated onion, minced parsley,
(½ t baking powder)

Leaving the peels on, wash and grate the potatoes, and then mix them with the remainder of the ingredients. Add an extra egg if the mixture is too stiff, and add more wheat germ if mixture is too wet.

Forming these into patties may be difficult. An alternative is to drop scoops of the mixture into a hot, oiled frying pan, flattening them with a spatula. Get them fairly thin (a half inch or less) so that the potato will cook through. Fry over moderate heat until brown on both sides. Serve hot, with cold applesauce or Cream Cheese Sauce.

Variations:
—Some mashed potato could be substituted for the raw potato, either in part or entirely.
—Add other vegetables: celery, carrot, mushrooms. The carrot and celery will cook best if they are grated or pre-sautéed. Since mushrooms cook more quickly, they can be sliced or minced and added raw.

For *Sunburgers*, omit the potatoes and wheat bran. Use 3 cups of sunflower seed meal, either purchased or home-ground. Mix the meal with grated or sautéed onion, salt and pepper, and enough egg to hold the mixture together. Mighty fine burgers!
—These could also be held together with mashed beans or potatoes.

Soyburgers

2 cups mashed, or blended, cooked soybeans; 1 cup cooked
rice, 1 onion, 1 carrot, 1 stalk celery, salt, pepper, 2 cloves
garlic, thyme, dill weed, 2 eggs, ½ cup wheat germ

Cut the vegetables very finely—mince or grate. (If left in larger pieces, sauté them before adding to the remainder of the ingredients.) Add more wheat germ if the mixture is not yet stiff enough to make into patties. Fry on both sides until well browned.

The patties could also be baked or broiled—turn once and brown on both sides. Serve with a white or brown sauce.

—*Lentils and barley* make a particularly good combination, replacing the rice, and *Oatmeal Soyburgers* are surprisingly tasty.

Condiments with Main Dishes

Serve a simple main dish with a variety of optional additions, which each individual may use according to his liking. Condiments make a meal interesting and fun, and their use need not be limited to curry dinners. Here are three of the almost endless possibilities.

Baked Potatoes

Serve baked potatoes with side dishes of butter, salt, pepper, sour cream, grated cheddar cheese, sliced green onions, chopped walnuts or cashews.

—Do the same with *Potato Cakes.*

Japanese Noodle Dinner

Cook the noodles until nearly done, drain, and place them in a big bowl or crock. Just before serving, pour boiling water over the noodles. Serve accompanied by Soy Sauce Broth (p. 177), raw or sliced hard-boiled eggs, sliced green onions, toasted sesame seeds, toasted nori (p. 105).

—The hot soy sauce broth could be poured over the noodles in place of the water.

Condiment Chef's Salad

Dress the lettuce or mixed greens and serve with an assortment of accompaniments: grated or thinly sliced vegetables such as radish, carrot, green onion, green pepper; fruits; toasted nuts; cheeses, either grated, cubed or sliced; sprouts; croutons; marinated beans.

—Leftover vegetables or spaghetti are good here also.

Planning Meals

Nothing left in the kitchen but a few odds and ends you have to dig out of the refrigerator? Faced with unlimited choice in a market? Either way, you have to take what's there. At first you dread it. Later you come to enjoy it.

Respond to each thing, each vegetable, each situation. More and more, start with what is actually there instead of with some pre-conceived notion. This is how a cook's real creativity and confidence are developed. Learning to tolerate more, to appreciate more, we learn to cook the way we want to, and to cook for others also.

Taking what's there and working with it includes making a tentative plan, a tentative menu. Once you get into it, it may change and you'll have to change, too.

What are the factors to consider in deciding on a menu? We have certain people to feed at a certain time (of day, weather, life), and we have certain foods available, certain time available for preparation, certain space available to work in. Also certain talent available. Don't sell yourself short on the latter by excluding everything you've never done before or everything you've had trouble with. Try making an honest assessment which still allows room to grow and to explore new and possibly difficult areas.

Next we'll want to consider what shape the vegetables are in. Vegetables which are no longer very fresh will probably be best cooked. Is there something which looks all right for a salad? Maybe the lettuce should be used today—while it is still usable. It's not necessary to use everything. Just enough.

As we begin deciding what to have, other factors enter in: How do the various dishes complement one another? In appearance? in texture? taste? feeling? To wind up with three gruels won't be very appetizing. Have some balance between simple and complex, dry and juicy, chewy and soft. And don't forget color. You aren't planning to serve potatoes, cauliflower with onions and white sauce, and tapioca pudding for dessert, are you?

What makes a dinner a dinner? Here are some ways to think about it. Let's say we have the following ingredients to start with: cheese, rice, tomato, lettuce, cabbage, onion, carrot, sunflower seeds and raisins. These, plus salt, pepper, oil, vinegar and possibly other seasonings.

Especially if we are used to eating meat, we will want a *main dish* to center the meal around. Other dishes on the menu are intended to complement this main dish and complete the "dining experience."

First of all, here's a *Casserole Dinner:*
Main Dish: cheese, tomato, rice
Vegetable: sautéed carrots with onion and sunflower seeds
Second Vegetable: steamed cabbage
Salad: lettuce with raisin garnish

Or a main dish of cheese, tomato, cabbage; sautéed carrots with sunflower seeds and raisins for the vegetables; rice as a side dish; and a lettuce salad.

Or how about a *Stuffed Vegetable Dinner:* tomato stuffed with rice, sunflower seeds and raisins; sautéed cabbage with onion and carrots; lettuce salad with grated cheese.

Or a tomato stuffed with cheese, rice, onion and carrots; sautéed cabbage; lettuce salad with sunflower seeds and raisins.

Or you could stuff the onions (or the cabbage leaves), serve the tomatoes in a salad or in a hot vegetable dish.

Another way to plan a meal is to plan it around a *staple*—a simple grain, potato or pasta dish. This is "home"—a plain taste from where we depart to have various experiences: sweet-sour, salty, rich, what have you. Periodically we can return home to have our taste renewed and refreshed for a further adventure. Home is generally low keyed and uninteresting so that we can get some rest there.

Here are some dinners created around a staple (rice), again using the same nine ingredients we started with:

Tomato with onion and carrots (sautéed); rice; cabbage salad with sunflower seeds and raisins.

Or carrots with onion and sunflower seeds; rice; cabbage salad with tomato and grated cheese.

Or onion with tomato and grated cheese; rice; thin-sliced cabbage and carrots with sunflower seeds and raisins.

Or cook the cabbage dish and consider adding a lettuce salad.

Rather than rice, the dinner could be centered around some plain cabbage:

Cabbage; fried rice with onion, carrots, raisins, sunflower seeds; lettuce salad with tomato and cheese.

Cabbage; rice with cheese and tomato sauce (with onion and carrots); lettuce with sunflower seeds and raisins for a salad.

The variations, permutations, elaborations go on and on.

By now it should be clear that a main dish dinner is well complemented with a plain dish, and that having a "home" dish doesn't exclude having a main dish too.

Once you've planned a menu, if you have any doubt about how to proceed, make a list of things to do in the order in which they need to be done. What's going to take the longest to cook? Leave yourself a margin for error, and be sure to do as much as you possibly can well ahead of time to avoid the last-minute rush. It's almost unavoidable, but keep trying. Have all the materials and implements at hand before you begin cooking. Put the vegetables in a sauce in a double boiler, or put them in the oven. Make up the salad dressing ahead of time.

Doing each step of the whole thing thoroughly, you will know when to stop.

Good Friends

Whatever cooking utensils you use, try to care for them and give them a home. Here are some suggestions regarding the care of two groups of kitchen utensils.

Wooden Items

Cutting Boards, Bread Boards, Salad and Chopping Bowls, Spoons, and So Forth:

Wood is alive—it absorbs and loses moisture, air, oils. With too much, or the wrong kind of, washing it will dry out and crack. Don't soak wooden implements or use soap to clean them.

On the other hand, with too little washing the wood will become gummy with a residue of oil and food particles. Wiping wooden bowls with a damp towel is often recommended, but sometimes they will need to be rinsed briefly with warm water, even scoured, and then wiped dry immediately.

Food particles and oil will inevitably build up on cutting boards, and then a vigorous scraping with a spatula helps. A scrub brush or soapless scouring pad can also be used to clean these surfaces, and vinegar, which has a mild bleaching effect, can be used in the scrubbing. For foaming action, sprinkle on some baking soda and then scrub with vinegar. Rinse thoroughly and wipe dry.

Wooden implements can be periodically oiled. Scrub off the residual build-up, and then apply light mineral oil (baby oil) sparingly, rubbing it in. (Vegetable oils will become rancid in the wood, and linseed oil isn't very good for you.)

Metal Pans

Cast Iron Skillets, Woks, Cookie Sheets, Bread Pans, and Other Baking Pans:
Proper care of these utensils will keep them from rusting, and also keep food from sticking. Here are the main points:

If new, or newly cleaned with soap or scouring, these implements should be "tempered," a process whereby a couple of layers of vegetable oil are cooked onto the pan. To temper, warm the pan on top of the stove or in a 300° oven for five minutes. Rub on the oil thinly and evenly, and then bake in a 300° oven for twenty to thirty minutes, or until the oil is browned. Repeat the application of oil, and then the baking.

Proper cleaning will keep this coating intact. Don't use soap or super-abrasive scouring pads when washing. Instead, use a brush or a plastic scouring pad to dislodge the food particles. If necessary, these implements can be soaked and then wiped or brushed clean.

Should a pan lose a significant portion of its oil coating, or get a gummy build-up on top of it, it is time for a thorough cleaning with soap, and then retempering.

Being Good Friends

"All students should be like milk and water. We are all friends from our past lives." —Suzuki-roshi

Cooking makes cleaning possible, cleaning makes cooking possible. It's all the same when we are good friends with ourselves and

241

with the world around us. To help us be good friends with ourselves and with others, with rice and cabbages, with pots and pans, we may need some rules:

Clean as you go.

Being good friends with the knives, clean and replace them in the knife rack after use.

Being good friends with the sponge, rinse and wring it out; with the towels, fold and hang them up, and wash when dirty, or before.

Being good friends with the counter, wipe it after use, and scrub sometimes; with the floor, sweep and mop. Get into the corners, and when you're done, stand the broom on end or hang it on a hook. After cleaning a greasy floor, sprinkle some salt where it's still slippery.

Being good friends with the dish sponge, don't use it on the floor. Use the dish towel for dishes, and have another for face and hands.

Being good friends with the scraps and trimmings, make some stock.

Clean the sinks! Clear the drains!

Be friends with your friends.

Index